Use What You Have®
Decorating

Use What You Have®
Decorating

Transform Your Home
in One Hour with
Ten Simple Design Principles—
Using The Space You Have,
The Things You Like,
The Budget You Choose

Lauri Ward

G. P. Putnam's Sons
New York

G. P. Putnam's Sons

Publishers Since 1838

a member of Penguin Putnam Inc.

375 Hudson Street

New York, NY 10014

Illustrations by Bill Crossan

Photographs on pages 24, 26, 104, 113, 136, 205, 206, 207
        by Tria Giovan

Additional photography by Lauri Ward

Use-What-You-Have® is a registered trademark of
Use-What-You-Have Interiors®

Library of Congress Cataloging-in-Publication Data

Ward, Lauri.
    Use what you have decorating : transform your home in one
hour with ten simple design principles using . . . / Lauri Ward.
        p.   cm.
    ISBN 0-399-14438-2
    1. Interior decoration—Handbooks, manuals, etc.   I. Title.
NK2115.W2   1998   98-14778   CIP
747—dc21

Printed in the United States of America

10 9 8 7 6 5 4 3 2 1

This book is printed on acid-free paper. ∞

BOOK DESIGN BY DEBORAH KERNER

To Joe and Tracy,

who have my heart and soul

With Gratitude

I am very thankful to the many people who have helped to make this book possible.

All of the Use-What-You-Have clients who have welcomed me into their homes and shared their decorating dilemmas and dreams, especially those kind (and brave!) enough to allow me to use the photographs taken at their consultations for these pages.

The "A" team, the talented trio whose excellence in their respective professions made this project so dynamic:

My extraordinary agent and new friend, Liv Blumer, who kept calling me after our first meeting because she knew it was time for this book to be written. Her intelligence, integrity, wisdom, and wit have guided and continually inspired me. I deeply appreciate the many things she has done to keep this book on track and on time.

I have great respect for my editor, John Duff, a true gentleman and brilliant editor. He structured my words and ideas like a literary architect with his inspired vision for this book. Our synchronous relationship enhanced every stage of our collaboration. I will always be grateful to him.

Everyone who has been involved with this project knows how much my husband, Joe Ward, contributed. He edited my writing, provided artwork, cured computer viruses, and wore so many hats that I can't imagine how we would have gotten along without his creative production skills and computer wizardry. As always, he has been there for me, filling my life with love and laughter.

Two sweet people, Jamie Raab—the godmother of this book—and Dennis Dalrymple, who have been so very supportive.

Bill Crossan, for his accurate illustrations and fine attention to detail, and Tria Giovan, whose skillful photography always captures the best in everything.

The talented people at Putnam:

The design team, whose work made my heart sing: Deborah Kerner, Isabella Fasciano, Lisa Amoroso, and Claire Vaccaro.

The very capable Lisa Beck, who went the distance with the book clubs, and Jill Bernstein, who handled subsidiary rights.

All of the dedicated Use-What-You-Have designers, especially Rita Grossman, my dear friend and the first designer trained in the Use-What-You-Have system, and the members of the Interior Refiners Network® for their loyalty, passion, and commitment to making people everywhere happier in their homes.

My assistants, Minal Patel in particular, who managed to decipher my scribbled writing, even when I couldn't.

All of the enthusiastic women around the country who attend my decorating seminars and make them so much fun.

Jennifer Unter, Joe Gramm, and Barney Karpfinger at the Karpfinger Agency for all their help.

My design idol, Andrée Putman, who told me always to remember how important humor is when decorating a home.

Literary agent Esther Newberg, who in the early 1980s was the first to suggest that I write a book.

My late mother, Hedy, father, David, and brother, Bobby, who I am sure are all watching and smiling down from above. And my late grandmother Lillian, who was always there for me.

My uncle Steven Chase, who provided childhood inspiration with his fabulous designs, and my old friend Regina Mayerfield, whose writing has always left me in a state of awe.

Finally, I am so grateful for my daughter, Tracy Taylor Ward, who brings me so much love and joy every day. I hope that she will continue to use everything God has given her to reach her full potential as she grows up, and throughout her life.

Special Acknowledgment

I want to express my deep appreciation to Susan Suffes. An accomplished editor and writer, her professionalism and organization helped to guide me and expedited this project immensely. Susan's expertise and sense of humor made working with her both instructive and fun. I have found her to be a kind, considerate, and spiritual soul.

From Valentine Avenue to Lexington Avenue, I'm glad our paths crossed. I will always be grateful to her for her help with this book.

Contents

Your Home: **A True Reflection of Who You Are**   1

Introduction: **You Are Not Alone**   3

Part 1:

**The Ten Most Common Decorating
Mistakes and How to Correct Them**   11

1   **Tell Me What You Want**   13

2   **Creating a Comfortable Conversation Area**   16

3   **Proper Furniture Placement**   42

4   **Finding Balance**   63

5   **Furniture of Different Heights**   80

6   **Creating a Cohesive Look**   88

7   **Finding the Focal Point**   97

8   **Using Artwork Effectively**   116

9   **Skillfully Displaying Your Accessories**   135

10 **Using Lighting Correctly**   160

Part 2:

Making Your Home Even More Beautiful   179

11 **The Shell**   181

12 **Live Well in Every Room**   200

The Don't Use What You Have Top Ten   219
Your Final ReWard   220
I'd Love to See Your Before-and-Afters   221
Sources   222
Index   224

"Do what you can,
with what you have,
where you are."

—Theodore Roosevelt

"We shape our dwellings,
and afterward, our dwellings shape us."

—Winston Churchill

"Your house is a place to keep your stuff,
while you go out to buy more stuff."

—George Carlin

A True Reflection of Who You Are

In our own ways, we all strive to reach our full potential: intellectually, spiritually, and physically. And more and more, the way we choose to live—and most of us are lucky enough to have many choices over our lifetimes—is an expression of who we are. Helping you to find that true expression is the purpose of this book. Because so many of us have become slaves to fashion and the expectations of others, it's often difficult to exercise the freedoms of choice we have and still create an environment that is comfortable, practical, and unique. Your home should be original, just like you. And when you learn to "use what you have," you will find the freedom to be yourself.

I believe that *everyone* deserves to have a lovely, restful home that is a comforting retreat. Most important, it should be fashioned from elements that have particular meaning to you. Your things—furnishings, collections, and accessories—are a unique combination that represents who you are. Those colorful prints on the wall remind you of a sun-splashed vacation in Mexico.

The old rocker in the corner that belonged to your grandmother holds special memories for you. The needlepoint rug in the foyer was the first purchase you made after you got married.

My personal philosophy never encourages the sentiment "Throw it all out and start over again!" If there is one fundamental precept that I would never abandon it is the notion that no one is a blank slate; we all have ideas about what we care for or what makes us feel uncomfortable. Your belongings define your own private world and their history merits respect. When you use what you have, your home truly mirrors who you are.

Of course in my own business and throughout this book, there are time-tested principles, tricks of the trade, and other tried-and-true ideas that can help you realize your own vision and self-expression. Learning these conventions is like knowing the basic rules of etiquette—once they are mastered you have the liberty to enjoy yourself without fear or anxiety. You will learn why things look and feel better one way or another. You'll come to understand why a room feels off kilter or simply uninviting. You will also learn the best lesson of all: You will learn to trust yourself.

You Are Not Alone

When I first started working as a conventional interior designer, I went into people's homes and told them how to create a new look by getting rid of all of their existing furnishings and selling them new furniture.

But unlike others in my field, I was willing to admit that I didn't feel comfortable with this scenario. Many of my clients had lovely furnishings; the problem was simply how they were being used. I knew that there had to be a sane alternative to starting over completely.

In 1981, I founded Use-What-You-Have Interiors® and began to offer my clients a new option that simplified interior design. Implementing change could be done on a large—or small—scale with ease. Creating a comfortable and beautiful home became an easy-to-achieve goal.

A client's personal style is paramount and deserves respect. It will always be my beacon because my philosophy isn't only about decorating, but about mindset. I work to assure every client that they don't have to be concerned about fads or fashion. My message is this: do what *you* like; find your focus and follow your heart and your instincts; don't be influenced by what your friends have or what your family thinks is attractive. *Don't look for anybody's approval but your own.*

As interior design consultants, my associates and I hear the response "I never would have thought of doing that!" from almost every person we work with. Next to the satisfaction of helping our clients realize their own special visions, it is probably the greatest compliment we could receive. It means that the Use-What-You-Have philosophy is working. For the last two decades, we have helped transform thousands of homes all over the country, from log cabins to condominiums to mansions. We've discovered that all of these clients share one common dilemma: they feel that their homes simply don't look or feel right, but they can't pinpoint what the problems are. And they not only want to correct the problems, they want their homes to be the best they can be.

My Clients: Their Stories

Some of my clients had already worked with interior designers. They'd spent huge sums of money, but, they told me, they didn't feel that their homes reflected who *they* really are. This never surprises me; after all, the professionals they hired encouraged them to buy new things, based as much on the decorator's taste as on their own (not to mention large commissions).

Other clients, just setting up their first homes, bought one piece of new furniture and suddenly realized that they didn't have a clue about how to pull a room together.

Lots of couples, who have come together in their thirties and forties, bring to their newly combined households a wide array of styles in furniture and art, some of which are significant investments. Each person loves their own belongings but realizes that they don't match their partner's things. Few, however, want to sacrifice their own past.

There are the couples who have just had a baby and may not be ready to buy a lot of new furniture, but they still want to have as lovely a home as possible while keeping safety and practicality in mind, too.

I've received many calls from people who need help with a house full of heirlooms they've inherited from their parents, and they don't know how to integrate them with their own possessions.

Then, there are the empty-nesters in their fifties and sixties, who are selling large houses after their children leave or, upon retirement, are moving to much smaller condos. They take the things that have meaning but they don't know what to do with them in their new homes. They need and want a simpler decorating style, but how to achieve it is just beyond their grasp.

There are the people who are relocated every few years by their companies to different parts of the country. Buying new furniture and accessories just isn't an option, either financially or emotionally: often their possessions are the only stabilizing elements in their lives.

And, of course, there are the people who move into new homes, where the rooms are different sizes, shapes, and configurations from what they're used to, and they just can't figure out what goes where, why, and, especially, how. They know what they like, but can't conceptualize the way things will look in their new space.

All of these people have something in common: *Each one is unconsciously making, at least one—and more often several—of the ten basic decorating mistakes.* Any one of these can cause lots of frustration, and a combination can be downright traumatic.

Decorating is like investing. Unwise choices can cost you money. Few people are really taught to understand and play the market. Fewer still have been trained in the principles of good interior decoration. For years, interior designers have kept these simple secrets of transforming a home to themselves. And with good reason: once the principles are known, anyone can apply them. I believe in and have put into practice a very easy-to-understand method that everyone can use. And I do mean everyone—no one need ever be excluded from having an attractive home because of limited budget or time.

This applies to someone renting a first apartment as well as to a wealthy homeowner. An old club chair and ottoman can be displayed with as much panache as a priceless antique collection.

To every one of my clients, and to you, I make this promise: your errors are quick and easy to fix. And that's what Use-What-You-Have decorating is all about.

I know you share many of the same problems because I've seen them over and over and over again. The most common decorating mistakes are just that—common—*because everyone makes them and they're simply unaware of it.*

The Ten Most Common Decorating Mistakes

Here they are, the ten missteps that can jar your eye, generate irritation, and make you feel uncomfortable in your own home.

1 Not defining your priorities

2 An uncomfortable conversation area

3 Poor furniture placement

4 A room that is off-balance

5 Furniture of different heights

6 A room that lacks a cohesive look

7 Ignoring the room's focal point

8 Improper use of artwork

9 Ineffective use of accessories

10 Using lighting incorrectly

The Key to Use-What-You-Have

Throughout this book, I'll share with you the challenges I confront every day—basic decorating errors. But in order to solve these problems, you need to recognize them first. The principles embodied in the following decorating solutions are simple and logical. Once you understand them you'll be able to apply them and make your home into the restful, comforting place it's just waiting to be.

Remember: All of the precious things in your home reflect who you are. You can use what you have to create the home you've always dreamed of.

The Hassle-free Way to Redo Your Home

I'm going to walk with you through every room in your home, and the two of us are going to redecorate it, together. We're going to have fun doing it, too—because we're going to identify the mistakes quickly and use only what *you* like to correct them. And you're going to get an extra added bonus— instant gratification!

Each of these common errors—and the underlying design principle—is covered in its own chapter. I use a wide array of living rooms as examples, many illustrated with before-and-after pictures, because the living room is the place with the most problems. (Of course, these principles apply to the other rooms in your home as well.)

Important Note: Most of the before-and-after illustrations are actual photographs of clients' homes, not carefully constructed magazinelike layouts. They're examples of real decorating transformations for real people. What's fun is that they demonstrate what amazing changes can be made in just an hour or two!

All of the before pictures have at least one commonly made decorating mistake. But, you'll notice that there are often other missteps in these examples as well. As you progress through the book, you'll begin to spot these other mistakes yourself. So, to help you find them in those pictures, I've listed what the slipups are, with the appropriate chapter references. And, to make it even easier, each one has a clue, too. In addition, I've included a "banished,

YOU CAN
HAVE THE
BEAUTIFUL
HOME YOU'VE
ALWAYS
WANTED.
YOU JUST
NEED TO
LEARN HOW
TO USE WHAT
YOU HAVE.

borrowed, and bought" list accompanying all of the after photos. It will tell you what we removed, brought in from other rooms, or needed to buy—and in most cases you'll find that very few purchases were necessary.

Maybe you've never worked with an interior designer before and believe that the only way to have a beautiful home is to invest tens of thousands of dollars in it. Or, possibly, you have worked with a decorator in the past but feel that your home still isn't "you." You might be concerned that you'll have to start over again. If so, stop your worrying.

With Use-What-You-Have as your personal guide, you can have a lovely home just by rearranging what you already own. The mistakes you inadvertently made in the past will become a faint memory—and you'll never make them again. And, if you want or need to add pieces, I'll show you what to buy to avoid costly mistakes.

If you've read a lot of decorating books that have not addressed your decorating dilemmas, don't be disheartened. As beautiful as they are, most of those books are based on particular styles. They can't necessarily solve the problems in your home, which are caused when design principles aren't applied correctly. Or perhaps you've searched furniture showrooms and stores, wondering if the pieces on display would work for you. Unfortunately, because stores are sales-oriented, and therefore not concerned with helping you correct existing design mistakes in your home, you've probably walked out confused and overwhelmed.

During the course of any consultation, my clients naturally ask me for advice about what to buy to enhance the aesthetics and value of their homes or to avoid making costly errors. My suggestions for accomplishing both of these goals, in the most economical, practical, and time-efficient ways, are featured throughout the book.

With Use-What-You-Have, you'll immediately see ways to improve your home, no matter what style furniture you own. You'll also see decorating magazines in a whole new light and understand why the layouts look the way they do.

Perhaps you think that redoing your home requires a lot of time, as well as effort, and the thought is nothing short of daunting. Relax. I know you have a hectic schedule.

With Use-What-You-Have, even the smallest change will make a dramatic difference. To accomplish these quick fixes, you can take the time that is convenient for you, whether it's an hour after dinner or an entire weekend. And, you'll see how everything fits together logically.

Throughout the book you'll see references to a ReWard, an instant reminder that the idea suggested has multiple benefits. Many times, when you fix one mistake, others will automatically be corrected as well.

Before You Start

I know that you want to get started right away. But before you begin to redecorate, please read the *entire* book. Doing so will give you the perspective of a *complete* consultation, and you'll see the logic and reasoning behind everything. Then, on the second go-round, if your time is really crunched, you'll be able to turn to the last page of each chapter, where you'll find a list of questions. These are the quick tips that you'll need for a one-hour room transformation.

Before you begin, you might like to take several snapshots of your rooms from different sides and corners. When you finish, reshoot the room from the same spots. You'll be amazed at the difference.

Miss Rumphius's Challenge

When my daughter, Tracy, was five, she was given a copy of Barbara Cooney's charming book *Miss Rumphius*. It is the story of a little girl who is told she must do three things in her life. The first is to travel to faraway places. The second is to have a house by the sea. And the third, and most important, is to somehow make the world a more beautiful place.

USING WHAT YOU HAVE PROPERLY IS THE MOST COST- AND TIME-EFFICIENT WAY TO FIX ANY DECORATING MISTAKE.

I consider it to be my personal mission to help make the world a more beautiful place—one house at a time.

With this book I hope you'll find lots of affordable new ideas to create the elegant and functional home you deserve. After reading it, you'll be able to use these techniques to make your own world a more beautiful place, too.

Once you become aware of what to look for, you'll see your home in an entirely new way. Help is right here, in your hands. So let's begin. Pick up this book and take it with you, from room to room. You're going to see how to pull together all of the elements in every area of your home. I promise: we'll take meaningful strides that will inspire you.

Once you see how simple and effective the solutions are, I bet your reaction will be, "I never would have thought of doing that!"

Part One

The Ten Most Common Decorating Mistakes and How to Correct Them

Chapter One

Tell Me What You Want

Your home says a lot about who you are. The things you cherish, collect, and love to display all deserve the best possible setting.

Most people with whom I've worked have the same goal. They want to have the loveliest and most comfortable home possible, no matter where they live, or what kind of home they inhabit.

But before any errors can be fixed, rooms transformed, or new purchases made, I always ask my clients to tell me what their needs and requirements are to help them determine their own priorities.

The Two Most Important Questions

1) Do You Own or Rent?

This is a simple yet vital question when it comes to establishing your priorities. In my capacity as a consultant, it immediately determines the approach I will take with a client, and it should help you in setting your own parameters as well.

If you are like most people who rent, you are not interested in investing in, and making substantial changes to, someone else's property. You are looking for simple and inexpensive ways to make your living space as pleasant and functional as your budget allows. The Use-What-You-Have approach is ideal, because it allows you to maximize what you already own without making major expenditures.

BY DEFINING

YOUR

PRIORITIES

YOU'LL BE

ABLE TO

ORGANIZE

AND PLAN.

If you own your home, whether it be a co-op, condo, or private house, you may very well want to invest more time and money in it. But, almost everyone has to work within a budget and wants to spend their money wisely. Use-What-You-Have decorating not only shows you how to do more for less, but how to get the best value for your money.

Or, you may be at the point of wanting or needing to sell your property. You are looking for a quick redo that will make a big impression on potential buyers. In just an hour or so, you can transform your home with the Use-What-You-Have principles.

2) Who Lives Here?

If you are a single person embarking on a new career, your needs will differ from those of a couple with a new baby. If your family consists of two adults and three children, your requirements will not be the same as those of a retired couple who have sold their big family home and moved into a much smaller condo.

If you love to entertain, your home needs to accommodate your lifestyle. Rooms may need to do double duty; furniture has to serve multiple purposes. If you travel a lot, either for business or pleasure, you want to come back to a tranquil, restful, and low-maintenance home.

Your Priority Questionnaire

Whatever your situation may be, nothing should be done randomly. Starting with this simple questionnaire will help you determine what's most important to you and how to achieve your goals.

- Do you rent or own your home?
- How many people inhabit the space?
- Do you have children? How old are they? Where do they do their homework?
- How long do you expect to live there?

- What kind of work do you do?
- What kind of work does your partner or spouse do?
- Do you or anyone else in your household work at home?
- Do you have pets? What kind?
- Do you entertain often? For how many?
- How large are the main rooms?
- What are the exposures?
- How are the rooms used, i.e., do they have multiple functions?
- How many people use the rooms?
- What is the condition of the walls and floors?
- What do you like about your rooms?
- What are your favorite pieces?
- What do you dislike about your rooms?
- What would you like to get rid of?
- Is there enough storage space?
- Where are the television, audio equipment, and computer located?
- How many places are there in your home where you can curl up and read?
- Are you comfortable?

As you go forward, keep your answers to these questions in mind. They will help you budget and stay focused on *your* goals.

Whether you own or rent and how long you plan to live in your present home will affect the amount of time and money you should spend. If you rent and plan to move within the next year, *don't* spend any money. Be content with moving your furniture around. If you own, however, every change you make can add to the resale value of your home. Remember, the needs of everyone in your household will also impact on the time and money you should spend on your living space. Your kids need a place to roughhouse; your widowed mother needs a place to rest . . .

Now that you have a clearer picture of what your needs are, let's go into your living room and take the first step to creating your new home.

Chapter Two

Creating a Comfortable Conversation Area

For many of us, the living room is the most important room in the house because it is highly trafficked and multipurposed. Throughout this book, I'll spend a lot of time in the living room, but the principles and ideas that are offered here will apply to all the rooms in your home.

Your living room should be seductive and comfortable. Rather than a showcase to be admired but never used, it should be accessible and cozy, a place of refuge.

For most people, the living room has always been defined by how it *looked*, instead of how comfortable and functional it was. How many houses do you remember (your own included) that reserved the living room as a museum for the "company" furniture. Or, worse, was it full of furniture covered with plastic to "protect" it? It's little wonder that so many people approach the task of doing the living room with such anxiety.

For others, family patterns are in evidence everywhere. For instance, was your father's favorite chair set off in a corner by itself (where he escaped into his newspaper every night), and does your own living room re-create the same setting? It's an important observation because it demonstrates one of the key principles in this book: the position of that chair, set off in the corner, put a "screaming distance" between your father and the rest of the family. But equally important, it leads you to ask the question: "Am I doing things in my own home because that's how they were done when I was growing up?" A family pattern, like history, has a habit of repeating itself, regardless of how uncomfortable, or impractical, it may be.

Today, you get to make your own choices. The dictates of fashion have been overthrown. Of course, there will always be the "look" of the moment—retro modern, country cluttered, shabby chic—but the principles of good design are timeless. And the desire for comfort and practicality is paramount.

Creating a Comfort Zone

Today, in most homes the living room serves many functions: it's a place to relax, to read, to listen to music, or to watch television. By turns, it can be a cozy corner in which to nap or the site for a killer round of Monopoly. If you are lucky enough to have a separate family room, then the living room can be reserved for entertaining. However, for many of us, the living room is the only meeting place for family or guests to come together.

The living room is the place where aesthetics really count. But it can be the most self-conscious place as well. Often, it's perceived as the hands-and-feet-off-or-else room. And because it is usually the largest room in a home, it not only has the most traffic but is filled with the most furniture—just because the space can hold it.

Whatever uses your living room may have and whatever furnishings may already be there, your primary goal will be to design a usable and inviting space. And the first step in accomplishing this goal is to create what is known as a "conversation area" around which every other function can be accommodated. Very simply, you want to arrange your furniture in a way that allows you to carry on a relaxed conversation.

In the pages ahead, you'll learn about the four goals of a conversation area. You'll see how you can eliminate the "screaming distance" that creates a barrier to comfortable interaction. You'll also discover many ways to redirect traffic patterns so that they make the room "work" better—for conversation and for many other uses.

GOOD

DESIGN MUST

BE BOTH

AESTHETICALLY

PLEASING

AND

FUNCTIONAL.

The Four Goals of a Conversation Area

1　To create a simple arrangement of furniture so that people can sit facing each other and can speak without raising their voices. Generally, the basic ingredients required to create the ideal conversation arrangement for a standard living room are a sofa, a piece of furniture serving as a coffee table (it can be an ottoman, for instance), and two upholstered chairs. There are alternatives, however, such as a pair of loveseats with a pair of chairs. But keep two things in mind: a) upholstered furniture is the most comfortable, and b) whatever the configuration, everyone seated should be able to reach the central coffee table.

　　If space allows, a secondary privacy area can be set up, which may consist of a desk and a chair, or a club chair and ottoman with a table and lamp next to it. Very large rooms can even hold back-to-back sofas or love seats, creating two separate and distinct conversation areas with the addition of chairs.

2　To establish a focal point in the room. A wall unit, fireplace (a real one, if you're lucky, or a fake one, if you can manage it), or even a grand piano can serve as the dominant fixture in the room, which helps orient the whole arrangement and gives you a visual reference point.

3　To eliminate traffic that runs *through* the conversation area (unless there is no alternative). In other words, the arrangement should be self-contained so that conversations will not be interrupted.

4　To free up space in the room for other functions, like a separate reading or working area. Once you establish a workable arrangement, the rest of the room begins to fall into place naturally—like finding the key piece in a complex jigsaw puzzle.

THE MUST-HAVES ■

Correcting a design mistake is easy, but to make your room the best it can be there are a few basic guidelines to follow. These are the "must-haves," those fundamentals that create the most comfortable conversation area possible. You probably already own most, if not all, of them. You need:

- An upholstered or leather sofa or two love seats

- Two upholstered armchairs

- Reading lamps

- A coffee table or piece of furniture that functions as one (an ottoman, a tray with legs, or a hinged wooden trunk, for instance)

- A small table in easy reach of the chairs, especially if the chairs are not part of the main conversation grouping

- 18" square throw pillows (at least two) for the sofa

A Before-and-After Story:

"Screaming Distance"

The 23' x 20' living room of Rachel and Joe's Denver home was their primary space for entertaining, which they did frequently with small groups of friends. It had plenty of comfortable seating, but the arrangement didn't lend itself to the kind of intimacy they wanted for their parties. In short, the room simply didn't work for them. The main problem here was that when everyone was seated, they had to raise their voices to be heard because the seats were spaced too far apart from one another. This is a classic and common error that I call "screaming distance." The room itself had some wonderful features: a fireplace, tall, elegant windows, well-placed entrance doors, and an overall well-proportioned shape. A staircase with graceful turned spindle railings filled the wall opposite the fireplace.

The sofa and three club chairs were all upholstered in the same floral fabric. The rectangular coffee table was convenient only to those seated on the sofa and on one chair. There were no other tables in the room. The other major piece of furniture was a large antique pine armoire that loomed large, dominating one entire wall.

Other Common Mistakes

- **Ignoring the room's focal point**

Clue: **Find the most interesting architectural element in this room.**

- **Ineffective use of accessories**

Clue: **Look at the top of the window.**

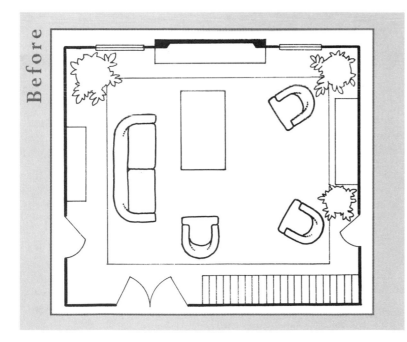

Before

Within an hour we had rearranged the room using the basic conversation-area principles. It felt, and looked, dramatically better. With the sofa and two chairs, we created a self-contained U shape, using the fireplace as the main focus and reflecting the symmetry of the flanking windows. (See chapter 7 for more on focal points.) The coffee table was centered so that it was now accessible to everyone. The third club chair was moved to a bedroom.

We were also able to address a few other problems by removing or rearranging objects and pieces of art that detracted from the clean lines of the room. (See chapters 8 and 9 for more about art and accessories.)

Now that the issue of screaming distance was corrected, every conversation, no matter how large the group, would feel more intimate.

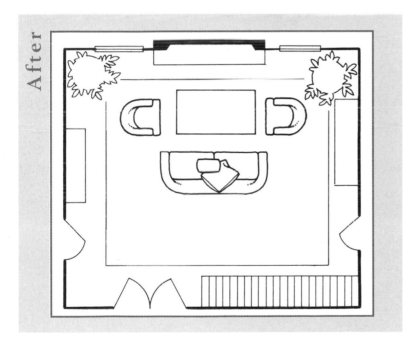

After

A Before-and-After Story:

Creating Flow

At first glance this 11' x 17' room seems to have a workable conversation area, but for Charles, the *look* of the living room in his new suburban Atlanta townhouse lacked style and flow. A bachelor, Charles called me after several frustrating attempts at rearranging his furniture in the new space. He was starting with good basics—clean lines, two large central windows, and built-in symmetrical bookshelves that flanked one window. Although the room wasn't very large, the furnishings were appropriate for the scale—a pair of slipcovered loveseats (one slightly smaller than the other), an antique coffee table, two interesting occasional chairs, and a number of eye-catching accessories. But the existing arrangement was completely rigid, and didn't show off either the furnishings or the accessories to their best advantage. The limited space seemed to restrict any major changes yet there was lots of room for improvement.

Even before we started working on the room, I noticed that one of the occasional chairs had a mate in the foyer. I'm a great believer in keeping couples together, so we carried the mate into the living room and moved the unmatched chair to the foyer.

Other Common Mistakes

- **Poor furniture placement**

Clue: **Look at the sofas.**

- **Improper use of artwork**

Clue: **Observe how high the painting is hung.**

- **Ineffective use of accessories**

Clue: **Check out the bookshelves.**

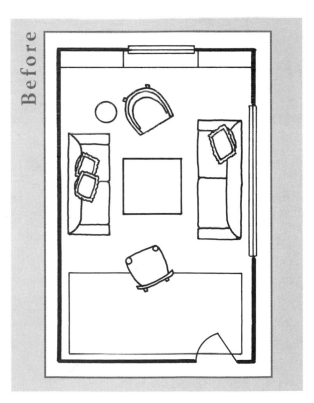

Before

The first challenge was to give the room a more re-laxed feeling. (See chapter 3 for more about furniture placement.) And because there actually was sufficient space, we were able to take the sofas off the wall and an-gle them, while still keeping them parallel to each other. The newly reunited matching chairs and coffee table followed suit. This arrangement enabled Charles to walk *around* the furniture comfortably and it eliminated the disruptive traffic pattern *through* the conversation area. Then we brought a brightly colored flat-weave rug in from the bedroom and placed it on top of the existing sisal rug, under the coffee table. This made a big difference in defining the area.

We also borrowed a standing lamp from the second bedroom, and finished the room by rearranging the accessories and art on his bookshelves and coffee table. (More about art and accessories in chapters 8 and 9.) In addition, we added a pedestal and a green plant from other rooms of the house. To complete the room, Charles purchased several large, patterned throw pillows in the same primary colors that were in the oil painting on the wall.

By simply looking at the room from a new perspective and applying several principles, we had created a room that was more comfortable *and* more stylish.

What We Banished

- An unmatched chair

What We Borrowed

- A matching chair
- A rug
- A lamp
- A pedestal
- A green plant

What We Bought

- Throw pillows

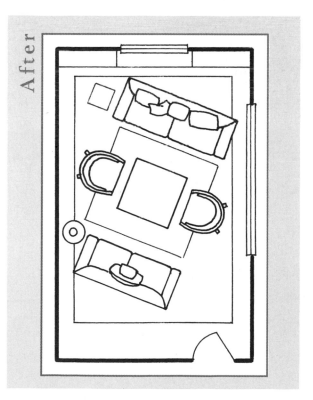

After

A Before-and-After Story:

Finding Your Center

Patricia was a single mother living with her son in a contemporary two-story townhouse in Cleveland. When I arrived at their home, she brought me into her living room, which had on one side sliding glass doors that led to a terrace and on the opposite wall a staircase that led to the dining room. In addition, a fireplace was centered on a small angled "fifth" wall.

Although she'd looked for an answer in decorating magazines and had tried various rearrangements, Patricia couldn't figure out how to create a comfortable conversation area in the awkwardly shaped 21' x 15' room.

An upholstered sofa was pushed against the long back wall (usually my place of choice for the biggest piece in a seating arrangement) and the matching loveseat floated in the middle of the room. They were "screaming distance" from each other, effectively killing any feeling of intimacy. Two ladder-back chairs (one out of view in the photo) were placed somewhat haphazardly in the room. A coffee table, against the wall near the fireplace, was cluttered with books, papers, and an oversized table lamp. A small wooden cube was used as a

Other Common Mistakes

- **Improper use of artwork**

Clue: **Look at the frames.**

- **Ineffective use of accessories**

Clue: **Check out the top of the mantel.**

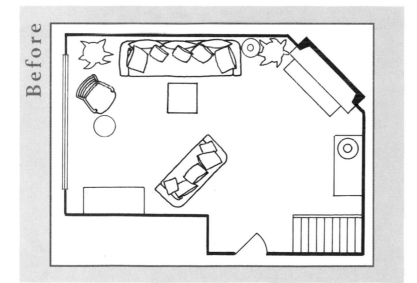

Before

makeshift coffee table. Finally, a couple of leggy dracaena trees filled the remaining wall space.

Although she had the necessary components for a conversation area, Patricia had ignored the awkwardly situated fireplace, which was her focal point. (See chapter 7 for more on focal points.)

We rearranged the room by first moving the sofa to face the mantel, with the loveseat at a right angle to it. One of the ladder-back chairs was added to create the third side of the conversation area. The coffee table, cleared of clutter, became the center of the grouping. The second chair remained in the corner near the window. We moved the table lamp to her son's bedroom and put the cube in the den. This instant makeover gave the room the cohesion and intimacy that was missing. We then reinforced the new focal point by moving the largest piece of artwork over the mantel (see chapter 8) which allowed the room's clean lines to work as a backdrop so that we could better display the accessories (see chapter 9).

On the wall adjacent to the sliding glass doors that are out of view, we left a cabinet that held all of Patricia's audio equipment. The wall to the right of the fireplace, with the staircase, was left unchanged.

For the first time, Patricia was able to have a cozy chat with her guests and watch a roaring fire, simultaneously.

What We Banished

- A table lamp
- A wooden cube
- One painting

What We Borrowed

- Nothing

What We Bought

- Nothing

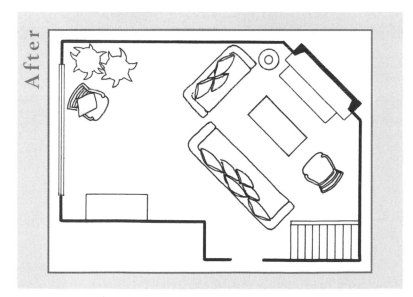

A Before-and-After Story:

Form and Function

Although most people complain about having too little space, sometimes a lot of room can seem like too much of a good thing. That was Emily's dilemma.

A widow, she lived in a large 1960s Fort Lauderdale condominium overlooking the Intracoastal Waterway. Her living room's corner location had fabulous, sunny views from big windows and a terrace.

Emily had tried to fill the 24' x 28' space by spreading her oversized furniture all around the room. She had placed her sofa at the far end, by a quadruple window, alongside one pine end table and ginger jar lamp. On the opposite side of the room, near the entrance, were three floral chairs (one is not visible in the photo) and a metal and glass end table that supported a column-shaped lamp. Floating in the middle of the room was a large, square, pine coffee table that was accessible only to those seated on the sofa and one chair.

As with many rooms I encounter, this one felt like a jig-saw puzzle with all of the pieces in the wrong place.

The key to Emily's puzzle was to, literally, pull her room together so that it could function better. Until her conversation area was established, she wouldn't be able to use much of the space for anything else.

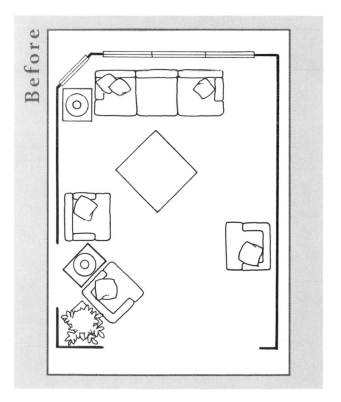

Before

Other Common Mistakes

- **Improper use of artwork**

Clue: **Note small picture floating on long wall.**

FLEXIBILITY EQUALS GOOD DESIGN. THE MORE DEFINED THE FUNCTION OF A ROOM IS, THE MORE YOU'LL ENJOY IT.

Creating a Comfortable Conversation Area

Even though Emily's living room was large, the first thing we did was sacrifice one of her oversized club chairs. (Three chairs in the same fabric were too much.) We then rearranged all of the other furniture so that the sofa was on the longest wall, in-between the windows, with the two remaining club chairs flanking it. The coffee table, which had been in the middle of the room at an awkward angle, was squared off and placed in the center to provide an anchor for this ideal conversation area. Mates to both the pine end table and column-shaped lamp were found in other rooms. We brought them in and created two sets of pairs, giving the arrangement balance and symmetry (see chapters 4 and 6). I also suggested that she buy a new 9' x 12' seagrass rug to go under the entire seating area. Later, to finish the room, a large horizontal oil painting would be purchased to hang above the sofa.

Having satisfied the room's basic requirement, it was now time to turn our attention to making the space more versatile. I recommended that Emily purchase a large wall unit and place it opposite the sofa. In addition to giving the new conversation area a focal point, it would house a television, lots of books, and all of her audio/video equipment. This addition would change the whole dynamic of the room.

What We Banished

- One upholstered armchair
- An unmatched table lamp

What We Borrowed

- A column-shaped lamp
- A pine end table

What We Bought

- A wall unit
- A rug
- An oil painting

A Before-and-After Story:

The Case of the Misplaced Coffee Table

Robert hadn't lived in his 1960s high-rise apartment in Chicago very long when he called me for help. Nothing looked or felt right to him. He recognized that his eclectic furnishings weren't being well used in this space.

Similar to many apartments of this era, this one featured a 21' x 16' living room with an L-shaped dining room, standard 8½' ceilings, parquet flooring, and large, if architecturally undistinguished, windows.

The first thing I noticed was the odd placement of the butler's table behind the sofa, which had been positioned in the middle of the room with its back to the main entranceway. The table was a lovely piece that deserved more attention. It needed to take center stage to become the anchor for the conversation area.

Other Common Mistakes

- **Poor furniture placement**

Clue: **The sofa and end table are creating a barrier.**

- **A room that is off-balance**

Clue: **Note the size of the furniture.**

- **Furniture of different heights**

Clue: **Look at the left wall.**

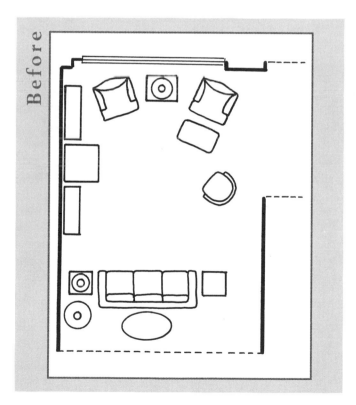

Before

The transformation began by rotating the seating arrangement 180 degrees. With the sofa in front of the window and the wing chairs opposite, the major visual and physical obstacle to the flow of the room was immediately eliminated. Next, we moved the butler's table in front of the sofa, where it would be accessible and become the centerpiece for the new conversation area. The upholstered ottoman was centered in front of the two chairs. The tall bookcases, which made the standard-height ceilings appear low, were moved to the entrance foyer, where they were placed side by side. A long console table was brought in from the dining area and placed behind the sofa to support a pair of celadon crackle-finish lamps. A couple of extraneous end tables and a chair were "banished," and an Oriental-style area rug was "borrowed" from another room to further define the newly configured arrangement. Later on, Robert had a low unit made for the long wall to house audio/video equipment.

What We Banished

- Two bookcases
- Two end tables
- A chair

What We Borrowed

- A rug
- A sofa table

What We Bought

- A low wall unit

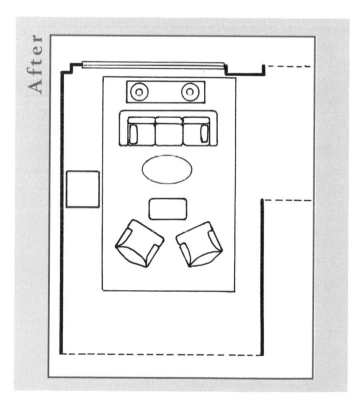

COFFEE TABLE FACTS ■

The coffee table is the centerpiece of every conversation area. In order to maximize comfort and function and minimize upkeep, consider the following:

- The average coffee table height is between 16" and 18" high. A good size for smaller spaces is 36" long by 24" wide. If you can't find a small table you like, consider using two small cubes or cylinders side by side.

- If you use your living room often, I recommend that a coffee table be made of either wood or metal, in any style you like. (Glass tables are fragile, more often than not have sharp edges, and show every fingerprint and smudge. Marble is practical and durable if it is filed and polished.)

- If you're buying a new coffee table, look for one that offers possible storage space such as a bottom shelf or drawer, or a complementary upholstered or leather ottoman, which opens for storage, can be topped with a brass or wood tray. (Some come with small wheels, or casters can be added, so that the piece can be moved easily.) A hinged trunk is also an option, especially the decorative antique variety. If you have a sleep sofa, a trunk provides storage space for bed linens.

Your Conversation Area Checklist

To create the most pleasing and comfortable conversation area that lets you talk without raising your voice, ask yourself if you have done the following:

- Positioned the sofa on the longest wall away from the entrance of the room?

- Placed two upholstered chairs facing or flanking the sofa?

- Set a coffee table between the sofa and chairs within easy reach of everyone?

- Arranged the sofa, loveseat, and a pair of chairs in a U shape, with the sofa on the long wall?

- Eliminated the need for anyone to have to twist in order to make eye contact?

- Used your area rug beneath the sofa and chairs to define the conversation area?

- Removed all extraneous furnishings?

- Made yourself more comfortable?

Chapter Three

Proper Furniture Placement

Time and again I hear clients say to me:

- "There just isn't any other way to arrange my furniture."

- "If I rearrange things, they just won't look right."

- "I've tried moving the living room furniture around every possible way I could think of, and it just never looks any better. It isn't very comfortable, either."

Chances are you've said these same things to yourself. There's one basic reason why you might feel unhappy with the arrangement you have, so I suggest that you take another good look at your living room right now with the following question in mind: Is all the furniture pressed against the walls?

Who can't recall a living room with all the big furnishings pressed against the walls? Lined up, one after the other, were end tables, sofas, armchairs, rockers, a piano, floor lamps. And let's not forget the wall units, armoires, bookcases, and various cabinets that may have stood side by side with them.

Do you remember how you felt in that room? Did it give you the same feeling you have in a doctor's waiting room? Was it easy to have a conversation in that room? How accessible was the coffee table? And even if the room was large, despite the space in the middle of the room, did you feel that the furniture was crowding you in, making you feel claustrophobic?

The inclination to turn furniture into "wallflowers" is, unfortunately, a tradition that has been passed down from generation to generation. Perhaps it made enormous sense when there was a fire in the middle of the living space. Today, however, there is absolutely no good reason to do so.

Pushing furniture—especially seating—up against the walls is one of the most common design mistakes that I encounter. Most people assume that this configuration will create the illusion of more space or allow them to put more furniture in their room. Others believe that it permits easier access into and out of the room. Ultimately, the only result is a "wallflower" room that feels uncomfortable and looks awkward.

And, unless the room is very tiny, it also lacks a comfortable conversation area (see chapter 2) and probably creates the roller-coaster effect (more about the roller coaster in chapter 5) with furniture of varying heights lined up against the wall.

Creating Fluid Traffic Patterns

In every room of your house you should be trying to create traffic patterns that let you enter and walk around the room with the most ease. Proper furniture placement may at first seem a complicated task, but all it really takes is common sense and learning to look at your rooms in a new way.

Consider, for instance, your kitchen or dining table. Are the table and chairs accessible from three or, preferably, from four sides? They probably are. What is true for your dining room or kitchen, should also be true for your living room seating.

Every room should invite you in, not stop you at the doorway before you enter it. It's important to create a path that flows in and out of the room easily. To make sure that you have the best traffic pattern possible for your space, take note of these points:

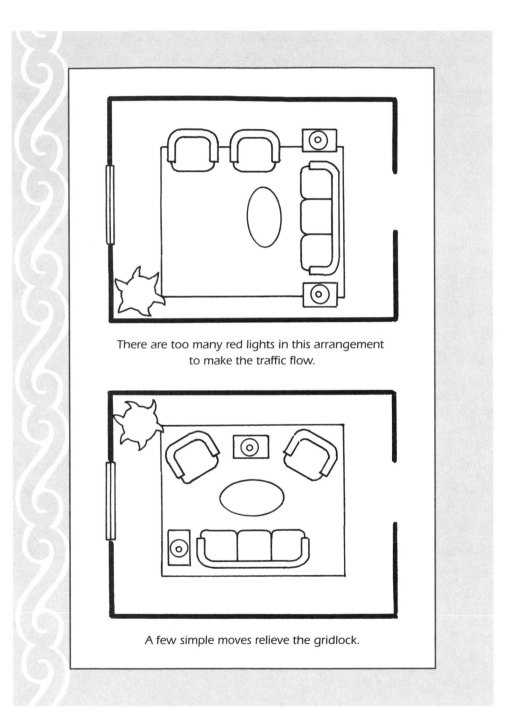

There are too many red lights in this arrangement
to make the traffic flow.

A few simple moves relieve the gridlock.

The location of your doorways: If there are two doors, consider having the traffic pattern move behind the seating, not through it, from one door to another. If there is only a single doorway, it's best to have easy access directly to the seating, as long as you leave enough room around the sides and behind it to move comfortably.

■

The placement of your major piece of furniture: If your sofa is placed off the wall, leave a minimum of 2½' to 3' of walking space *behind* it. A bit less space is needed in between chairs and the sofa.

■

The seating arrangement: If you have a long wall, establish your seating arrangement there, with the sofa against the wall as the anchor. Traffic will flow around it.

■

Obstructions: If a sofa or chair is obstructing a doorway, it must be moved.

■

Lethal weapons: Sharp edges on coffee tables or end tables force you to slow down or even swerve to avoid hitting them. Using round, oval, or rectangular pieces with rounded corners will contribute to a safer, more comfortable flow.

■

Limited space: If the room is small, you may only be able to walk around the room on one path, but as long as you can access the sofa and chairs easily, you will achieve your goal.

A Before-and-After Story:

The Wallflower Dilemma

Jim and Laura, and their two small children, had been living in this New England house for many years when they decided that their living room needed a new look.

"What can we do here?" Laura asked me. "We like our furniture and the fabric, but, to tell you the truth, it just doesn't look very attractive the way it is. With the kids being so young, we don't want to invest in all new furniture."

Their solid blue sofa, a pair of large patterned club chairs, and a television all hugged the walls of their 15' x 19' living room. A narrow coffee table, flanked by two little white chairs in the center of the room, was used by their children. In addition, a small bookcase and an end table were pressed into the corners of the room. A 6' x 9' patterned rug was laid on top of the hardwood floors. Three paintings were hung haphazardly on the walls.

The traffic pattern flowed in an endless circle around the coffee table and kiddie chairs. The furniture placement made it impossible to carry on a conversation above the din of the children in the center, the sound of the television, and the interference by anyone who was literally walking around the room.

Other Common Mistakes

- **Ignoring the room's focal point**

Clue: **What do you enjoy looking at?**

- **Improper use of artwork**

Clue: **Is your eye drawn to the art?**

- **Using lighting incorrectly**

Clue: **Do these lamps work together?**

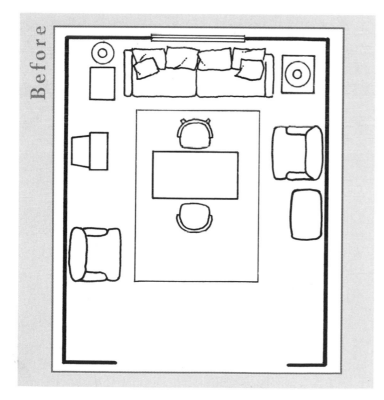

Before

To make the room more comfortable and practical, we moved the sofa to a long wall and placed the two chairs adjacent to it and facing one another. The coffee table was centered between the chairs to complete the conversation area. It wasn't difficult to persuade Jim and Laura to move the children's chairs and toys back into their bedroom, as they were happy to reclaim the space.

The end table, with its lamp, was placed next to the sofa. And, as a temporary measure, the small bookcase was positioned at the other end of the sofa, where it served as a second end table. (Later on, they would purchase another matching end table and lamp.)

Across from the sofa, where the television formerly stood on a rolling cart, a wall unit was earmarked to hold books, audio/video equipment, and family photos.

Finishing touches included simple replacement and positioning of lighting fixtures (see chapter 10), creating a focal point with the wall unit opposite the new conversation area (see chapter 7), and grouping the artwork (see chapter 8).

By pulling the furniture off the walls, we redirected the traffic pattern so that it was possible to walk through the room without obstructing conversation in the now self-contained seating area, while enhancing the overall aesthetics.

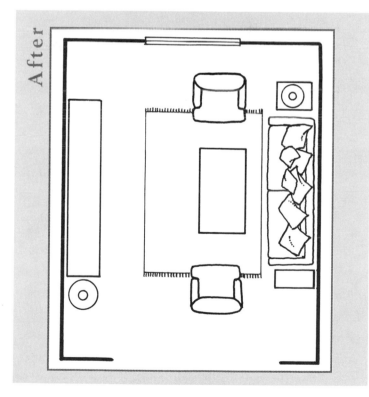

What We Banished

- **Two kiddie chairs and toys**

What We Borrowed

- **Nothing**

What We Bought

- **Matching end table**
- **Matching lamp**
- **Wall unit**

A Before-and-After Story:

A Modular Dead End

Steven and Barbara, a couple in their late twenties, had been recently relocated to Baltimore. Their modern three-bedroom apartment didn't have any distinguishing architectural features but it did boast 9½' ceilings and beautiful herringbone wood floors. The 15' x 21' living room had one large window at the far end, across from the entrance to the room. On the left wall, near the large archway into the room, stood a tall armoire. Opposite it, on the right wall, was a 1916 baby grand piano. Straight ahead, under the window, was a beige leather modular seating unit that extended to the left wall in an L shape. A coffee table was also placed against the left wall, and a small end table was tucked into the corner in-between the modular pieces. A simple wheat-colored sisal rug lay in the middle of the room. In addition, a built-in storage cabinet under the window enclosed the air-conditioning and heating units.

Having all of the furniture pressed against the walls was not conducive to easy conversation because no matter where you sat, you had to twist your head—or body—to face the person next to you. (Long L-shaped configurations, whether they are made up of modular pieces or a loveseat and sofa combination, always foster uncomfortable conversation.)

Other Common Mistakes

- **Uncomfortable conversation area**

Clue: Are there any seating pieces that face each other?

- **Improper use of artwork**

Clue: Are the two paintings next to the window necessary?

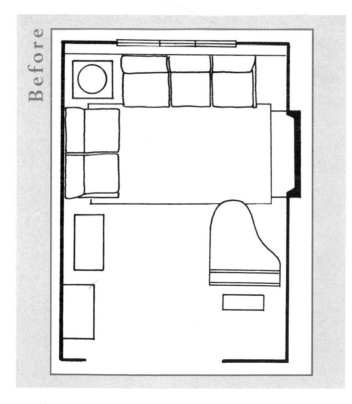

Before

To begin, we reconfigured the modular sofa so that three of the pieces, on the long left wall, created a "sofa" under the large oil painting on the longest wall (ReWard: This rearrangement reinforced the painting as the focal point of the room.)

The two remaining armless sections were moved to the opposite side of the room and placed on angles facing the sofa. The coffee table was then centered among the three pieces where everyone could easily reach it. This new arrangement enhanced the traffic pattern, permitted access to the built-in storage units, and, most important, allowed people to face each other comfortably while seated—an arrangement that is as functional as it is attractive.

To soften the overall look of the room, I suggested slip-covering the upholstered pieces. As it happened, cream-colored slipcovers with black piping had already been made and used in their previous home but were set aside in the chaos of moving. Within an hour, the room had been pulled together into a configuration so versatile that it could be used around almost any focal point we chose to make—a window, fireplace, or wall unit (see chapter 7). In this case, the painting became the focal point. We also repositioned some of the artwork to complement both the existing furnishings and the clean lines of the room (see chapter 8). Later, Steven and Barbara purchased a few accent pillows and a black chenille throw.

What We Banished

- **A small end table**
- **Two paintings**

What We Borrowed

- **Nothing**

What We Bought

- **Accent pillows**
- **Chenille throw**

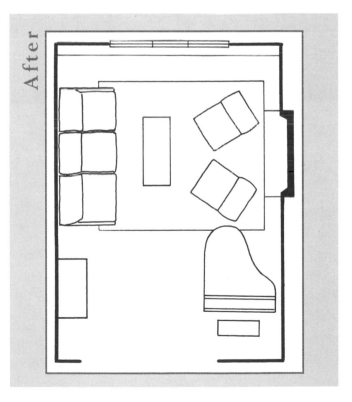

After

The Walk-through Living Room

Judy and Mike lived in a center hall colonial in New Jersey. Their large 24' x 19' living room, used for entertaining, reading, and listening to music, had a small archway that led in from the foyer at the front end of the house. The room was architecturally interesting, with its fireplace, bay window, and wall of sliding glass doors that led to a rock garden.

The navy blue sofa was on the long wall flanked by a large, round, plaid-skirted table and a drop-leaf table. At the far end of the room stood a grand piano by the sliding glass doors. At the opposite end of the room, under a bay window, sat a pair of pale yellow patterned club chairs. A Provincial settee jutted into the room, adjacent to the fireplace.

Diagonally across the room from the small archway was another doorway into the family room, which was used mainly for watching television. In order to get there, one had to walk across the entire living room and in-between all of the furniture, thereby disturbing anyone seated in the room. The only way to correct this problem and enhance the room aesthetically would be to establish a new traffic pattern.

To create a more harmonious flow into and through the room, we began by removing the large, round, skirted table to an upstairs bedroom. Our next step was to move the sofa into the center of the room facing the fireplace, with the two yellow club chairs flanking it. The coffee table was placed in the center of the group. This created a self-contained seating area that would not be disturbed by the traffic through the room.

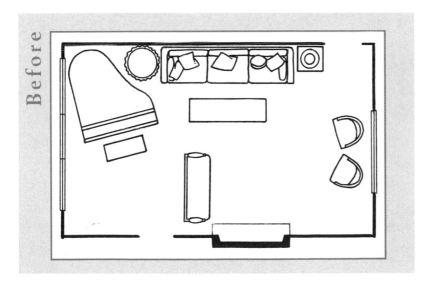

Before

Other Common Mistakes

- **A room that is off-balance**

Clue: Take a look at the tables.

- **A room that lacks a cohesive look**

Clue: Do you see any pairs?

- **Ignoring the room's focal point**

Clue: What is most dramatic in this room?

- **Improper use of artwork**

Clue: Which pieces should be removed?

As long as your room is wide enough, it is perfectly fine to have a sofa or loveseat at a 90-degree angle from a wall or centered in a room, provided that the back of the piece looks good. You might consider placing a long console table, with a pair of lamps, at the back of the sofa.

In many cases, especially where the living and dining rooms are combined, this arrangement will define the boundary between the two, but you still have to ensure that you're not disrupting the traffic pattern by creating an obstacle course or blocking a doorway.

We then placed the drop-leaf table, which had been used as a sofa end table, in the center of the long wall where the sofa formerly stood. We opened its leaves and collected framed photos from all over the downstairs rooms to create a mini-gallery. This gallery could be viewed by everyone walking on the path in front of it and behind the sofa.

In addition, the settee was then moved to the small wall across from the piano so that guests would have a place to sit and listen to music. We also carried in Judy's mother's antique desk from the dining room and placed it in front of the bay window so that she could enjoy the view while doing her correspondence.

Finishing touches included removing and regrouping much of the art on the back wall. We also created a display area for Judy's most treasured objects on the glass shelves to the left of the fireplace. A pair of sterling candelabra now flanked an oil painting over the mantel, and an heirloom clock was centered on the antique desk. (The candelabra and clock were originally in the dining room.)

What We Banished

- Skirted table
- Excess art

What We Borrowed

- Antique desk
- Heirloom clock
- Pair of candelabra

What We Bought

- Nothing

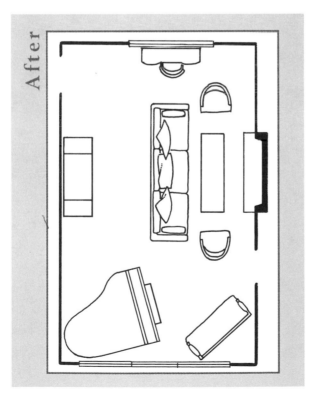

A Before-and-After Story:

Dining in
the Comfort Zone

The Bensons owned a small, stucco California house which has a long, narrow (20' x 12') dining room. They were passionate collectors of the early-twentieth-century Viennese furniture of Josef Hoffmann. Although they loved the style, they complained that it was difficult to arrange the pieces they owned in the space they had. We immediately identified the main functional problem: it was awkward to move in and out of the upholstered bench at the dining room table. Two of the dining chairs had been abandoned at the far end of the room. In addition, the round pull-up side tables (one is out of view on the left) were not being utilized properly. The dangerous sharp corners on the glass dining table also contributed to the lack of comfort.

Aesthetically, the Hoffmann furniture more than satisfied the Bensons, but the challenge was to make their collection as functional as it was handsome.

Other Common Mistakes

- **Ineffective use of accessories**

Clue: **Look at the bookcases in the upper left corner.**

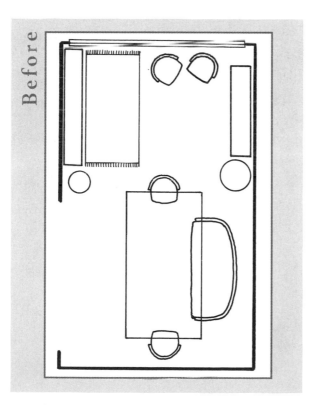

Before

As it turned out, a simple rearrangement was all that was necessary. First, we removed the pair of chairs by the sliding glass doors. In their place, we centered the bench that was formerly at the dining room table. The larger round pull-up table now served as a coffee table. The smaller round table, placed alongside one of the glass-fronted bookcases, was used to hold extra serving dishes for entertaining. We then encircled the table with all of the chairs. We removed the small rug near the sliding glass doors, rearranged the books and objects in both bookcases, and hung a group of prints from another room on the long wall above the dining table. (See chapters 8 and 9 for more on art and accessories.) Later, the corners of the glass table were completely rounded.

   With these simple moves, the room now had a more cohesive look as well as more functionality.

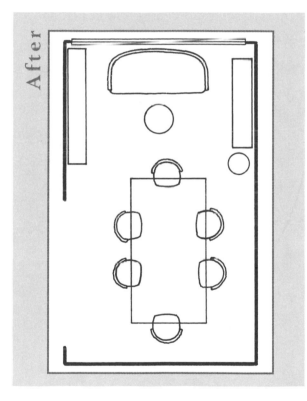

Your Furniture Placement Checklist

To make sure that you have eliminated the "line-up" in your room and enhanced both its function and comfort, consider the following:

- Is the sofa or loveseat against the longest wall? Or, if at a right angle to the wall, does it define the living space or anchor a conversation area without creating obstacles to traffic flow?

- If you own both a sofa and loveseat, is the sofa placed against the longest wall with the loveseat at a right angle to it? Have you added one or two chairs on the opposite side to complete the grouping?

- If you own a sectional or modular unit, have you configured it to facilitate the flow of traffic through the room?

- Are your occasional chairs positioned "off the walls" and facing each other or part of a U-shaped arrangement with a sofa or loveseat?

- Have you removed any excess pieces, such as unneeded end tables?

Chapter Four

Finding Balance

In the early part of the twentieth century, there was a prevailing look in women's fashion—huge, elaborately decorated picture hats worn with long, narrow skirts. When I see old pictures of these women, I imagine them tottering off into the sunset using every ounce of their strength to keep themselves upright. About the same time, people were living in houses overfurnished to the point of claustrophobia—heavily brocaded, dark, and forbidding.

Whether it's in clothes or home furnishings, we can easily recognize the tyranny of fashion. But it's not always the particular style that is the problem. Those big hats were gorgeous; the slim line of the dresses bespoke elegance. But most women just couldn't carry it off. And in that small Victorian parlor filled with heavy Victorian furniture, all those weighty pieces crowded into a tiny space overthrew the room. (But we don't have to go back a full century to see how fashion got the better of us—the 1950s saw the popularization of interiors awash with skinny-legged chairs and tables, giving us the impression that the whole room would just walk away!) More often than not, it is a matter of balance not of style.

The balance of a room is affected by both the placement of furniture *and* the size of each piece. If all of the big pieces are crowded to one side of the room, it will be off-balance horizontally. If much of the furniture is either too bottom heavy or too top heavy, a room will be off-balance vertically.

Balance is a problem for everyone—and a challenge, too.

At the outset, we have to keep in mind that all rooms are bottom heavy simply because all of the furniture is sitting *on the floor.* If you own a very large sofa, inherited your father's enormous desk, or bought a massive bombé chest at an auction, you have a lot of weight on the floor that needs to be "lightened" up. Conversely, if your grandmother's rocker is sitting between two spindly piecrust tables with narrow pedestal legs, then you need to add some "weight."

Measure for Measure

To allow you to use your furnishings in the best way possible, you not only have to consider the style and color of the major elements—sofas, chairs, tables, and other large pieces—but also the proportion of these pieces, so that they can be balanced by considering the width, height, and weight. Once you have determined how these components will work best, you can use accessories, artwork, and combinations of other small pieces to achieve the kind of balance and harmony that will bring the whole room together.

Starting with the biggest pieces, you will want to look at each with an eye to its actual size and the visual space it fills.

Sofas and loveseats: As the largest piece of furniture in most living rooms the sofa or loveseat generally carries the most weight and bulk. Measure the width and depth of yours—whether it's one you now own or one you're thinking of buying—to the *outside* dimensions. You will also need to record the height of the piece, from the floor to the top of the seat back. These measurements will let you determine where a large piece can be placed without having to move it around. More importantly, it will give you measurements to compare with other pieces of furniture that you may wish to buy. Having measurements on hand also helps when you are purchasing slipcovers, rugs, or even a painting.

But even sofas or loveseats of equal dimensions may occupy dissimilar "visual" space. A piece with rolled arms, full tufted back, an skirted bottom will *look* heavier than one that has slim arms, a tight back, and exposed legs, even though they may be the same size. You will have to consider the look of every piece that you put into a room in terms balancing each.

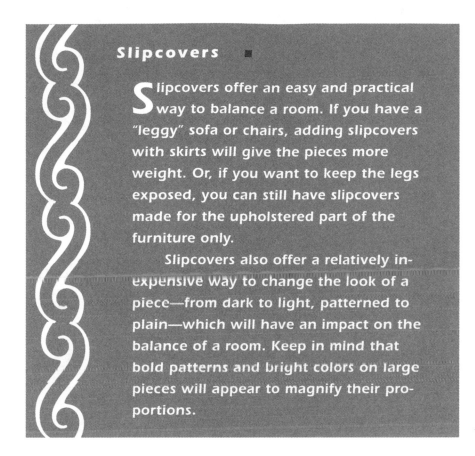

Slipcovers ■

Slipcovers offer an easy and practical way to balance a room. If you have a "leggy" sofa or chairs, adding slipcovers with skirts will give the pieces more weight. Or, if you want to keep the legs exposed, you can still have slipcovers made for the upholstered part of the furniture only.

Slipcovers also offer a relatively inexpensive way to change the look of a piece—from dark to light, patterned to plain—which will have an impact on the balance of a room. Keep in mind that bold patterns and bright colors on large pieces will appear to magnify their proportions.

Chairs: If you are working with a traditional arrangement of furnishings—sofa or loveseat and occasional chairs—the simplest way to achieve balance is to combine two matching or complementary chairs with the sofa or loveseat. Two smallish club or slipper chairs will be easier to arrange than one oversized chair or a "chair-and-a-half." Fully upholstered chairs are ideal for the main seating areas. Wooden chairs are best used as additional seating as needed. (Unless you have a very large room, your best option is smaller-scale pieces. But you do not want to accumulate lots of spindly, small chairs that could end up looking chaotic.) Depending on the size of your living room, once you have set up a conversation area (see chapter 2) you may wish to add a larger chair and ottoman in a corner to create a secondary seating area—the place where you can curl up with a good book!

Style and Comfort ■

As important as it is to achieve balance in a room, it is equally important to balance style and comfort. Sofas and loveseats with rolled arms offer a lot of style and comfort, inviting heads to lie down on pillows and cushions. Conversely, sofas with high, rigid, straight arms that force one's body into an awkward L shape are difficult to snuggle up on. But even the hardest-edged pieces can be softened with cushions and throws. Just because you like a contemporary look doesn't mean it has to be uncomfortable. There are plenty of options from which to choose and lots of ways to make any style as inviting to sit on as it is to look at.

The width of chairs is not as critical a factor as the width of a sofa when you are trying to create a balanced arrangement, but it is very important that the chairs and sofa be of approximately the same height—no more than five inches difference when measured from the floor to the top of the backs. If you have tall chairs, such as wing backs, which are often much higher than most contemporary sofas, you will have to make sure that a pair of these will balance each other or that you introduce some other element to keep the look relatively even. [ReWard: By keeping the height of your seating fairly consistent, you will immediately avoid creating a mini–roller coaster (see chapter 5).]

End tables: The third major player in the balancing act is the end table. The end table is the unsung workhorse of home decoration, since it has to be as functional as it is attractive. Your selection of end tables should take into account the same factors discussed for sofas and chairs because they can provide the means to find balance in the room—as well as a place to put stuff.

End tables should be no more than 2½" higher, or lower, than the arms of the sofas or chairs.

If the sofa and chairs are unskirted (their legs are showing), end tables should provide weight. Small legs or none at all, drum-style tables, or enclosed pieces such as small chests with drawers or shelves make the perfect complement to lighter upholstered furnishings.

A solid coffee table such as a trunk can be offset by more delicate end tables to avoid a bottom-heavy look.

Bookcases, chests, armoires, wall units: Other large pieces of furniture in your rooms can also have a dramatic impact on the balance, especially large, enclosed entertainment centers that are so popular today. Their sheer size often demands that they occupy prominent places. For the most part, one of these big pieces will be the focal point of a room (see chapter 7) around which most of the other furnishings can be arranged. They can often be balanced by the sofa or the largest piece of upholstered furniture.

The effect of a single tall bookcase, for example, can be made to appear wider by flanking it with artwork or other accessories. Any open-shelved unit should be arranged to eliminate clutter (see chapter 9 for more about arranging bookshelves, etc.) that can be distracting and contribute to an off-balance look. Two tall pieces can offset each other when positioned on the opposite sides of the room.

A Before-and-After Story:

Knocking Out the Heavyweight

Regina and Sam, a couple who married in their thirties, brought their respective furnishings to their new home, a modern condominium in Los Angeles. Their 21' x 12' living room was wonderfully symmetrical. It had a pair of windows that flanked a fireplace, and the opposite wall was completely filled with windows where a baby grand piano, an ottoman, and a decorative pedestal were situated.

The furniture, while a mix of styles and fabrics, wasn't completely at odds. However, everything was pushed up against the long side walls in parallel lines, crowded around the fireplace.

The camel-colored sectional sofa, along with a square Lucite table, had been Sam's before they were married. Regina's contribution to the living room was a pair of rather top-heavy tufted chairs with large rolled arms and thin chrome legs. With the weight of all the heavy furniture squeezed together, the room looked so off-balance that I had the impression if you opened up the fireplace wall, everything would go sliding out!

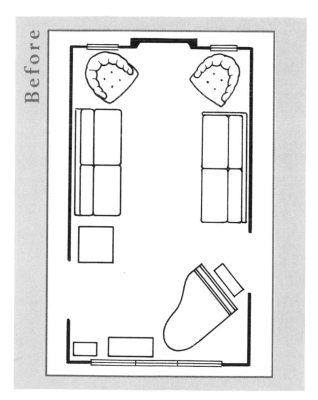

Before

Other Common Mistakes

- **Uncomfortable conversation area**

Clue: **The open "promenade" between the furniture might be appropriate for line dancing, but how easy is it to carry on an intimate discussion?**

- **Ignoring a room's focal point**

Clue: **What's the most eye-catching architectural element in the room?**

Finding Balance

It's amazing how effective even small changes can be. By simply creating a U-shaped conversation area, the weight of the furniture was evenly distributed around the room. The chairs were placed across from the fireplace, and their width was now balanced by the broad mantel as well as the sectional sofa on the side walls. The piano on the other end of the room was turned so that it was flush to the wall. This allowed more open space behind the chairs for a comfortable path into the sunroom. A matching ottoman on wheels, which had been on the opposite side of the room by the wall of windows, was moved in front of the fireplace for additional seating. The Lucite table was centered in-between the sofas to serve temporarily as a coffee table until a more appropriate piece could be purchased.

A floor plant, a chenille throw, and two pillows were brought in from the den to give the room a more finished look.

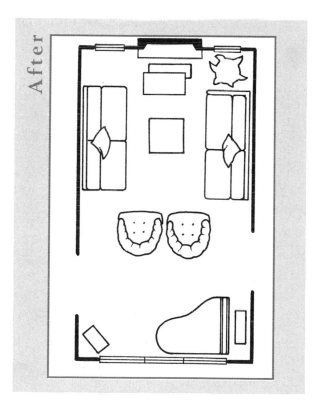

What We Banished

- **Dried-flower arrangement by the fireplace**

What We Borrowed

- **A floor plant**
- **A chenille throw**
- **Two pillows**

What We Bought

- **Nothing**

ReWard:

BY PLACING THE PILLOWS WITH THEIR POINTS UP, YOU INSTANTLY CREATE A VERTICAL LINE IN THE ROOM THAT DRAWS THE EYE UPWARD AND LIGHTENS THE OVERALL EFFECT OF THE HEAVY FURNITURE.

Finding Balance

TO ALL WOMEN WHO LIVE WITH DECORATING-PHOBIC, CHANGE-RESISTANT, IT'S-GOOD-THE-WAY-IT-IS MEN ■

I guess there's some truth to the idea that women and men really are different, after all. At least that's my opinion when it comes to decorating—an opinion founded on many years of working in this field and supported by the comments of many colleagues. Fundamentally, women seem to embrace change so it's not surprising that almost 90% of the calls my office receives are from women.

Consider fashion. Most women welcome the infinite clothing choices that are available to them. They can wear faded jeans and a T-shirt in the morning, a tailored suit in the afternoon, and a slinky black dress at night. Millions of women read fashion magazines to tap into the latest trends because they love style and variety.

Men, on the other hand, wear pretty much the same uniforms throughout their lives. Suits, or sports jackets and slacks during the week, jeans or khakis on weekends. End of story.

That brings us to decorating. Show a woman a sofa or a bed, and she'll have a great time adding as many throw pillows as she can in different shapes, sizes, and textures.

Point out the same sofa or bed to a man, and he'll start removing those pillows as fast as he can, wondering why in the world she put them there in the first place.

Ask a woman what shade of green she's thinking of, and she'll give you a full spectrum of choices, from seafoam to forest, olive to sage. Ask a man the same thing and he'll say green. Just green.

Most women seek change. Most men avoid it like the plague.

HERE'S WHAT YOU CAN DO ▪

If you're a woman reading this book you're probably eager to learn how to remedy your design problems. You know something is not working—that's why you're here with me now. Here's the solution: when you're ready to begin redecorating your rooms, let your man know that all of the ten design mistakes impact on his comfort. Once you make the changes, give him a day or two to get used to them. When he realizes how much better your home feels and how comfortable he is, he'll thank you.

A Before-and-After Story:

Musical Chairs

Naomi and Ken, a couple in their early forties, enjoyed entertaining in their elegant Arlington, Virginia, house. The 19' x 17' living room featured a fireplace flanked by low built-in bookcases. A large archway on the wall across from the fireplace led to a study. Handsome French doors on one side of the room provided access to the out-doors, and opposite, a second, smaller archway led to the dining room.

Two large skirted sofas flanking the fireplace were pressed against opposite walls while several wooden chairs were scattered around the other side of the room. A spindle-back bench was situated in the midst of the chairs across from the mantel, and a stack of nesting tables was placed beside one of the sofas. A small rug was centered amongst the furnishings on the hardwood floor.

Although the room had lovely architectural features, the couple complained that the room never felt very comfortable.

Before

Other Common Mistakes

- **Uncomfortable conversation area**

 Clue: **Is it possible to have an intimate chat in this room?**

- **Poor furniture placement**

 Clue: **Does the furniture have to hug the walls?**

- **Improper use of artwork**

 Clue: **Look at the height of the paintings.**

- **Ineffective use of accessories**

 Clue: **Look at the shelves.**

Naomi and Ken started out with the right idea. They had placed their sofas across from one another around the fireplace to create a focal point, and the beginnings of a workable conversation area. But the "sea" of wooden chairs at one end of the room didn't balance the heavy sofas at the other. In order to offset the weight of the upholstered furnishings, we decided to *remove* some of the leggier chairs. After moving the sofas off the walls to bring them closer together (see chapter 2 for information on creating a comfortable conversation area) we centered the long-legged, stacked nesting tables in-between the sofas and pulled them slightly apart to function as a coffee table. Now, the legginess of the tables was balanced by the solid weight of the sofas. We did leave two chairs with upholstered seats in the middle of the room, on an angle, across from the fireplace. The pair of chairs contributed visually to the balance of the room. Finally, the rug, which was too small to provide an anchor for the rearrangement, was removed to let the expanse of the gleaming hardwood floor contribute to the cohesiveness of the room.

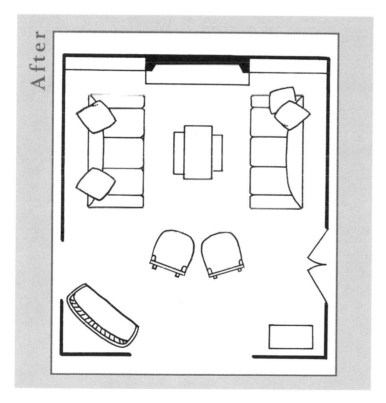

What We Banished

- Wooden chairs
- A rug
- Two prints
- Extraneous accessories and other items from the shelves
- Extra throw pillows

What We Borrowed

- African art

What We Bought

- Nothing

Once the primary task of achieving balance was completed, we were able to address some of the other flaws. Two prints were taken off the side walls, and the oil painting over the mantel was lowered three inches. (See chapter 9 for the proper way to display art.) Everything—except for the African art—was removed from the bookcases. From other rooms in the house, we gathered more wooden carvings and displayed the entire collection on the open shelves. (See chapter 9 for effective use of accessories.)

Last, we removed all the throw pillows except for four, large, floral squares, which were placed on the sofa with their points up. Doing so emphasized the African art on the shelves.

By reducing the number of leggy wooden pieces, and then integrating the remaining pair of partially upholstered chairs with the heavier furniture throughout the room, we achieved a balance, giving the space a more solid, tranquil, and elegant appearance.

Your Balance Checklist

To bring balance and stability to your room, consider the following:

- How does the height, width, and depth of each major piece relate to the other furnishings and their placement in the room?

- Are the upholstered pieces of similar height? (The difference in height between sofas and chairs should be no more than 5".)

- Does the mix of styles of your various seating pieces contribute to the overall balance of the room—or is everything bottom heavy or too leggy?

- Are the end tables no more than 2½" higher or lower than the arms of the sofa or loveseat? Does the style of these tables offset the weight of the seating?

- Have you balanced a lone vertical piece (i.e., a wall unit, armoire, or bookcase) with another tall piece of art or accessories?

- Have you used accessories—such as throw pillows placed with the points up—to create vertical lines?

- Does your arrangement make you feel calm and comfortable?

Chapter Five

Furniture of Different Heights

Even if you have followed the guidelines that I've set out in the previous chapters, you may still feel that something is wrong with your room but you can't pinpoint what it is. There is a very simple reason why your efforts may not have worked: the arrangement of your furniture, art, and accessories may be creating the dreaded—and very common—"roller coaster" effect.

Is There a Roller Coaster in Your Home?

The fastest way to discover if you have a roller coaster is to take a "ride" around your room—with your eyes. By learning how to really "see" a room, you can quickly determine what the problem is and solve it. Unfortunately, we often can't see what's right under our noses until it's pointed out to us.

So now is the time to share one of my tricks of the trade with you. It's a simple technique that only requires keen observation, like learning to read an X ray. Once you know what to look for, you can isolate the problem and determine a solution.

Isolating the Walls

Stand in the center of the room and face one wall.

Working from left to right (or right to left, if you prefer) take a long, slow overview of the entire wall. As your eyes scan the first wall, ask yourself the following questions:

Look at each element on or against the wall (with particular attention to the tops of pieces) and ask yourself these questions:

- Are my eyes being drawn up and down by the furniture, the art, the doors, and the windows because they are all different heights?

- Is there only one high vertical piece of furniture on the wall? If there is more than one, are they different heights?

- Is there a piece of art on the wall? How high or low is it hung in relation to other furniture, doors, windows, etc. If there is more than one piece of art, are these hung at different levels?

- Are accessories—flower arrangements, plants, or other decorative pieces—of unequal height?

- How do the doorways and windows fit into the overall arrangement? Do their heights differ?

Follow the same procedure on the three remaining walls. Make sure you take in every element on or against each wall.

Draw an imaginary line linking the tops of every piece around the room. (Do you see the roller coaster, or is the line softly undulating or relatively even?)

At this point, you should note the placement of the *highest* pieces of furniture in the entire room. Do they balance each other? If you have only one very tall piece of furniture, does it stand all by itself or is it adjacent to a very low piece?

Are the main furnishings—sofa, loveseat, and chairs—of similar heights or do they differ more than 5"?

Are the low pieces in the room about the same height or do they differ dramatically?

Is there a hanging light fixture that is either too large or too small or hung at a level that creates another "bump" in your line of vision?

A Before-and-After Story:

Surviving
a Coney Island Ride

I found a classic example of a roller coaster run rampant in
the living room of a large brick house in suburban Maryland.
When the MacIntyres moved into this home, they loved all
the space and the large, high windows which brought in lots
of light. A tall and wide arch led from the hallway into the 18'
x 22' living room. The long wall, opposite, featured a tradi-

tional brick-fronted mantel against dark wood paneling. A small archway adjacent to the fireplace led to a sunroom. Big windows dominated the third wall.

The room was furnished with a traditional floral sofa, a pair of solid white upholstered club chairs, a wing chair and ottoman, a brass coffee table, and two wooden end tables with brass lamps as well as a lot of art. Although the MacIntyres tried to give the room a warm, cozy look, the arrangement of the furniture and the placement of the art caused a very obvious problem—the roller-coaster effect.

To help them correct their problem, I showed the MacIntyres how to isolate their walls so that they could identify what was making them feel uncomfortable. Beginning at the top of the sunroom door, we followed the imaginary line as it rolled down to the fireplace, up to the large oil painting above

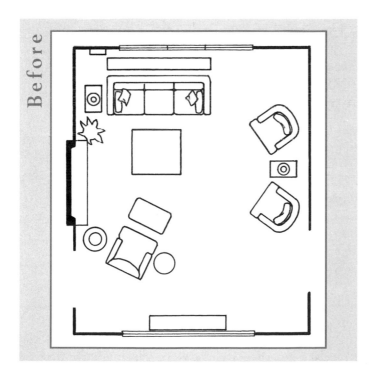

Before

Other Common Mistakes

- **Uncomfortable conversation area**

  Clue: Can more than two people chat easily here?

- **A room that is off-balance**

  Clue: Look at the wing chair and the sofa.

- **Ignoring the room's focal point**

  Clue: What's the most important architectural element in the room?

- **Improper use of artwork**

  Clue: Observe the corner.

- **Ineffective use of accessories**

  Clue: Can you see the photographs behind the sofa easily?

Furniture of Different Heights

it, and then down to the smaller painting on the right. We continued up again to two more prints and then farther still to the top of the large window. After a sudden drop to take in the low club chairs, we climbed again to see the uppermost curve of the archway. A few more stomach jolting bumps over the lamps, and the visual tour of the room left us all reeling.

■

By "isolating the walls" and following the imaginary line up and down the path of the furniture, art, and accessories as well as the doors and windows, the MacIntyres immediately understood what was making them feel uneasy.

Once everyone regained their equilibrium, a quick re-arrangement was all that was needed. First, the tallest piece of upholstered furniture, the wing chair, was tucked into a corner by the window with the standing lamp and small table—away from the rest of the seating—to minimize the difference in height from the other pieces. Then, the sofa was positioned in the center of the room, facing the fireplace. The two white club chairs were placed adjacent to the sofa, facing each other. In the center of this U-shaped arrangement, the coffee table provided the anchor for the conversation area. (See chapter 2 for more on comfortable conversation arrangements.) The end tables, with their matching lamps, were set next to the club chairs to complete the arrangement and to reinforce a balanced look to the room. (See chapter 4 for more on balance.)

What We Banished

- **Small paintings**

What We Borrowed

- **Nothing**

What We Bought

- **Nothing**

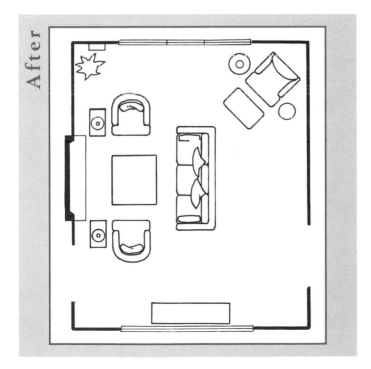

After

With the furniture rearranged appropriately, we turned to the artwork, which was one of the main culprits in creating the roller-coaster effect. The large painting above the fireplace became a strong focal point when we flanked it with several brass candlesticks that had been scattered around the room. It was also taken off the wall and propped on the mantel to bring it down a few inches. (The placement of the painting and accessories also helped to make the arrangement appear wider to balance the width of the fireplace.) The small paintings on the paneled wall were moved into other rooms in the house. (See chapters 7 and 8 for more about focal points and artwork.)

Accessories, including a collection of photos, were grouped on the coffee table and end tables so that they could be displayed without creating visual distractions. (See chapter 9 for tips on displaying accessories.)

Later, the MacIntyres whitewashed the fireplace and the paneled wall to brighten up the room.

With these simple touches, we were able to create an essential conversation area, balance the room, and eliminate the unsettling roller coaster.

If you are planning to purchase a wall unit, custom-made or not, take into account the architectural considerations of the room, particularly with regard to height. The standard height for wall units is 7'. Even if your ceilings are extremely high, don't immediately order a very tall piece. The higher the piece, the harder it will be to avoid the roller coaster effect and to balance it on the other side of the room with other furnishings. And, if you move, it may not fit into another room.

Your Roller Coaster Checklist

To keep a roller coaster from taking over your room, ask yourself if you have done the following:

- Isolated the walls? Stand in the center of the room and identify, one wall at a time, all the vertical furnishings and features.

- Considered the height of the tops of the doorways and windows? If they are exceptionally high, or vary greatly, can you compensate with tall furniture or well placed artwork?

- Checked to see if the main upholstered pieces of furniture are approximately the same height? If not, can they be arranged to minimize the up-and-down visual effect from one piece to another?

- Noted the presence of one very tall piece in the room? Can it be balanced with another piece or with a tree, a screen, or an arrangement of art?

- Balanced two tall pieces of furniture by placing them on opposite walls diagonally across from each other?

- Made sure that the lamps and accessories are of similar or equal height? Standard lamps need to be balanced—two on either side of a sofa or room should do the job.

- Eliminated the up-and-down pattern of artwork on the walls by rearranging, removing, or replacing the pieces?

- Made yourself more comfortable?

Creating a Cohesive Look

Nature loves pairs. Your own body—two eyes, two ears, two arms, two legs—is designed for stability and balance. In your home, whether it's large pieces of upholstered furniture, tables, lamps, small accessories, or works of art, pairs create harmony to which we naturally respond. Pairs help to establish visual rhythm in a room, too, as pleasant as a familiar melody. As you've seen throughout the book, bringing pairs together is a simple yet effective way to solve many basic problems. (Just think where Noah would be without his pairs!) We've paired occasional chairs to create a conversation area, we've arranged furniture of similar height to eliminate the roller coaster effect, and we've matched pieces for weight and size to achieve balance.

Pairs create instant cohesion. A lone plant, a single candlestick, a small photo hung in the middle of a long wall—each needs a mate. It is ideal, but not absolutely necessary, to have an identical twin. A complementary piece will make the image whole.

Pairs not only will add balance and cohesion to your room, they will contribute to the overall order of the space, which will make you feel more relaxed and comfortable.

In decorating, as in nature, balance is necessary, but it never needs to be boring. There are as many ways to add interest to a room as there are decorating styles, but first you need to establish a solid foundation that holds everything together. Once this fundamental principle of symmetry is integrated into your decor, your rooms will instantly have a more harmonious look and feel. And in most cases you can simply use what you have.

Adding Pairs to Your Home

Thumb through any good decorating magazine and you'll see pairs everywhere: two pedestals with urns, or matching vases brimming with flowers, twin oversized club chairs flanking a fireplace, duplicate mirrors behind a pair of consoles, a couple of andirons, double bookcases, two trees in matching planters. These items haven't been placed haphazardly or accidentally. The designers took careful inventory of these rooms to figure out how best to integrate pairs into the decor, achieving the cohesive look that makes these rooms work so well. And you can do this, too.

To begin, I want you to repeat the exercise from the previous chapter: isolate the walls. Now that you know how to look at a room, you can go through every room in the house: living room, dining room, foyer or entry way, and even the bathroom. The possibilities are endless. For instance:

- If you have two pieces of art, such as botanical prints or black-and-white photos that are the same size, create a pair by putting them in matching frames.
- Give your foyer symmetry with a pair of chairs (extras from the dining room?) flanking a chest.
- Hang matching sconces on either side of a painting or framed mirror.
- In the bathroom, hang an accent towel between a pair of matching hand towels.
- Lay a pair of complementary runners on either side of your bed in lieu of wall-to-wall carpeting.

The pairs displayed in this foyer create harmony and balance.

Throughout your home, you'll probably find pairs that haven't been introduced or that have been separated. I realize that sometimes it's impractical, or impossible, to find the twin of an existing piece, so the next best thing, of course, is to try to make the best use of whatever you already have.

For instance:

- Look for a double of your loveseat, or club chair, if you need more seating in your living room. You don't need an exact duplicate; a piece similar in height and size will do. Matching slipcovers can help make a pair, as can reupholstering if the furniture needs it (ReWard: When you put a newly created pair of chairs together with a sofa or other upholstered piece, you will have a complete conversation area.)

- Use two pairs of matching throw pillows on the sofa. I recommend that they be 18" squares, one pair in a fabric to match the sofa, the other in a solid accent color, perhaps from your chairs. (ReWard: When you set these pillows, with their points up, they provide a visual lift to the whole room.)

- Mismatched end tables or bedside tables can be finished in a complementary paint or stain to create the look of pairs.

- Tables of the same shape or finish flanking a bed, sofa, or loveseat will suggest a pair.

- A quick search around the house will turn up any number of accessories, from lamps to candlesticks to paintings or prints, that can be paired effectively.

A Before-and-After Story:

Creating
Two of a Kind

The Clintons (no, not *those* Clintons) lived in a Manhattan high-rise on the eighteenth floor. As in many modern apartments, the 20' x 15' living room had no particular distinguishing architectural details, other than the large windows that provided the perfect backdrop against which to create a wonderful room. The couple's sophisticated yet eclectic taste in furnishings—they mixed modern and antique pieces in various styles—made it a real challenge to bring harmony to the space. Two different sofas, plus a large square country French coffee table, two end tables, and a Chinese screen were all fighting with one another, so that the whole room lacked cohesion.

■

Following a good, careful look at the room to determine where things went wrong—and what was right—we started the transformation by switching the "end tables" and turning the taller, narrow chest so that its decorative door was hidden and only the plain wood side was visible. This way, its country

- **Improper use of artwork**

Clue: **Does the art help to create a cohesive look?**

- **Ineffective use of accessories**

Clue: **Do the mismatched lamps, books, and photos make the place feel homey or simply cluttered?**

- **Using lighting incorrectly**

Clue: **Look at the table lamps.**

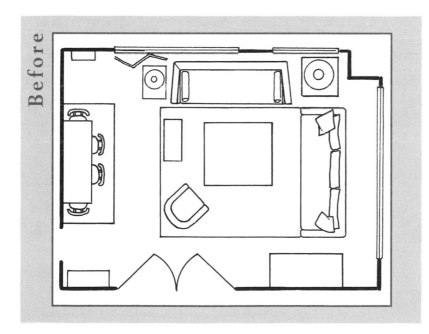

Before

style no longer clashed with the more formal coffee table and second end table. Because these pieces were all made of the same type of wood, they worked together. A pair of lamps that had been separated (one in the living room, the other in the bedroom) were brought together and made compatible by raising one on a stack of books so that they were of equal heights. (See chapter 5 for more on balancing heights.) We then switched the pillows on both sofas so that the colors were integrated, thereby visually tying the two largest upholstered pieces together. The simple addition of two candlesticks (from the dining room) in a complementary color added even more symmetry. (The Chinese screen—which was not being used effectively in this setting—was moved out of the living room and into the dining area to hide an air-conditioning unit. And the small pieces of artwork and the mirror were removed to give the walls a cleaner, uncluttered look. (See chapter 8 for more on hanging art.) By making a few quick adjustments we instantly created several pairs and eliminated some of the conflicting elements to give the Clintons' living room a more cohesive look.

What We Banished

- **Chinese screen**
- **Artwork/mirror**

What We Borrowed

- **A lamp**
- **A pair of candlesticks**

What We Bought

- **Nothing**

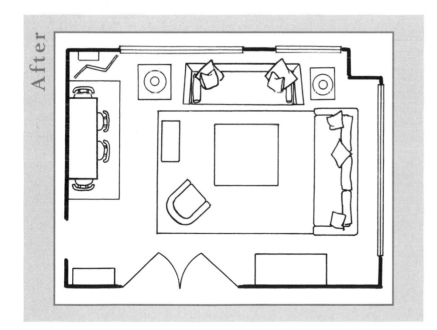

After

Your "Pairs" Checklist

To pull your room "together," ask yourself if you have done the following:

- Isolated the walls to determine where pairs could be used to create symmetry?

- Searched your home for pairs: chairs, tables, lamps, pieces of art, photos, or other accessories?

- Added a matching loveseat or club chair to create a pair? (If not, do you have two pieces of approximately the same height and size that can be slipcovered, reupholstered, stained, or painted to make them two of a kind?)

- Considered placing two pairs of 18" square throw pillows on the sofa to add symmetry and interest?

- Made yourself more comfortable?

Chapter Seven

Finding the Focal Point

No matter what your personal style or how beautiful your furnishings may be, every room needs a fixed point around which everything else will revolve. The area should be the most defined, striking, eye-catching spot in a room.

Whether it's the most obvious architectural feature in the room, such as a fireplace or French doors that lead to a garden or terrace, or a significant piece of furniture, such as a wall unit, the focal point provides a visual anchor that helps hold the room together. In some situations you may create a focal point with the right combination of furnishings and accessories—the sofa against the wall with a large painting above it—but simply grouping furniture together in one place will not give you that anchor. Neither will even the most elaborate moldings or a gorgeous chandelier. (As beautiful and eye-catching as these elements are, they generally draw the eye away from the central feature of the room.) Whatever elements or furnishings help to establish your focal point, to be truly effective, they must be positioned on or against a wall facing your conversation area.

Throughout this book, we have been addressing focal points implicitly as we created conversation areas (generally set against the longest wall) or dealt with the problems of furniture placement, balance, and cohesion. When we worked with pairs in chapter 6, for instance, by flanking a large painting with matching candlesticks or placing a chest between two chairs in the foyer, we created focal points. But the quest to find the perfect focus should begin by looking at what the room already has to offer.

Finding the Natural Focal Point

In a room stripped bare of furniture, there may be an obvious architectural feature that can become the ideal focal point: a large window or glass door (French or sliding) are probably the most common. But it is a fireplace that most people immediately acknowledge as the natural centerpiece for any room.

Since the discovery of fire, the hearth has been the traditional center of the home. Before central heating, furniture in the living room was automatically placed close to the fireplace for heat. Today, the fireplace (or even the fake mantel with electric logs) is an irresistible draw. But it's important to reinforce its role as the focal point. A large piece of art hung above the mantel—or propped on the mantelpiece if you don't want it hanging too high—is an ideal way to enhance the fireplace. Keep the accessories on the mantel simple and balanced, like a pair of candlestick lamps. I recommend that you keep the walls on either side of the fireplace free of artwork so as not to distract from it. If the fireplace is small, however, you may consider flanking it with a pair of pedestals topped with urns filled with flowers or dried branches, giving it breadth and weight and highlighting it as the centerpiece of the room.

Many houses and apartments are not blessed with fireplaces, but every home has windows. A large window or glass door—especially one that affords a great view—will override an interior focal point every time. If privacy isn't an issue for you, and the window frame is in good condition, use a very simple window treatment to let the scenery outside help decorate your room. (If your nighttime vista is particularly outstanding, remember not to light the window area directly since you'll only detract from the view.)

Don't worry about balancing two focal points in the same room. If you are lucky enough to have both a fireplace *and* a spectacular view, the view should take precedence. Realistically, whichever architectural point is the most dramatic will naturally dominate, but it is not a problem if you have more than one.

The simple elegance of a striking painting and a pair of candlesticks helps make the fireplace a strong focal point for this room.

A Room with No View

So many modern apartments lack significant architectural features. I think immediately of the rather featureless high-rises of the 1960s and 1970s that present their own particular challenges. Most don't have fireplaces and the vast majority have less than spectacular views. But you don't need to be discouraged because you can create a focal point by using just what you have.

In chapter 2, we looked at a number of ways to create conversation areas. Since I often recommend that the sofa be placed on the longest wall of the room, it's an easy place to establish your focal point. Hanging a large painting or framed mirror above the sofa immediately draws attention to this area. The weight of the sofa and the visual appeal of a large object on the wall serve the same function as a decorated fireplace or a big window with a view.

The throw pillows on this sofa literally "point up" the focal point of this room.

You can reinforce this effect with matching tables and lamps flanking the sofa or sconces on the walls that balance the overall arrangement as they direct the eye to the central pieces of the focal point. (We'll talk more about accessories and lighting in later chapters.) The key is to make a dramatic yet harmonious statement.

A popular addition to contemporary living rooms is the versatile wall unit. Not only does it serve as a place to house books and entertainment equipment, it can also become a viable focal point. Besides adding welcome closed storage space, open shelving with a lively arrangement of books, photos, and other objects (more about this in chapter 9) will give this piece the kind of impact it needs to become the visual anchor for the room.

Once you have defined your focal point, be sure that you don't distract from it. A good 3' to 4' of unadorned blank wall space on either side is the simplest way to ensure its full impact. But if you must add furniture, lamps, or other accessories to the area, be sure that these are paired and balanced so that they do not distract from the object of your focus.

ReWard

If you place two pairs of throw pillows on the sofa, one pair with their points up, they will create a vertical line to balance the other pieces of the same height in the room, carry the eye up and away from the heaviness of the sofa, contribute to the overall symmetry, and accentuate the painting or mirror above.

A Before-and-After Story:

Screen Gems

In spite of the wonderful big and airy space, beautiful furnishings, and interesting accessories, the owners of this Soho loft complained that their living room area lacked elegance, a description usually reserved for a more traditional setting. I recognized that it would be easy to achieve the look that eluded them because they had already followed many of the basic principles of good design. They had a comfortable conversation area and reasonably good furniture placement, but there was something missing. The room had no strong visual anchor. The dominant piece, the dark four-panel screen, created a black hole rather than providing a dramatic centerpiece that the room demanded.

What we needed to do here was to fine-tune the arrangement into a well-proportioned, balanced, and harmonious whole—the very definition of elegance—composed around an eye-catching focus. Without a well-established focal point, whatever else we did to the room would just be dressing.

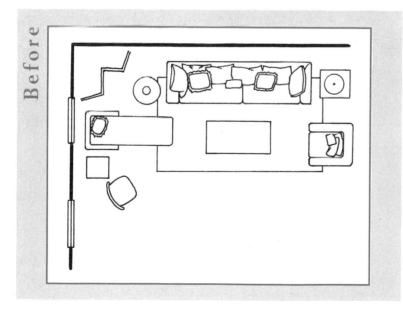

Before

Other Common Mistakes

- **A room that is off-balance**

Clue: **Note the *weight* of the screen.**

- **Furniture of different heights**

Clue: **Note the *height* of the screen compared to other furnishings.**

At first glance, it appears that the rearrangement of the furniture makes the real difference here. In fact, the most significant change was the replacement of the black screen with a more dramatic painted one that instantly became the center of attention. The spaciousness of this loft enabled us to pivot the conversation area into the corner, with the screen at the center, so that it became more inviting and visually more arresting. We placed the classically inspired bust behind the sofa against the backdrop of the screen to subtly reinforce this new focal point while adding the drama and elegance the owners were seeking. The addition of two stylish wrought-iron metal sconces on the adjacent walls balanced the screen and broadened its impact.

The arrangement of flowers on the round side table, the standing lamp, and the bust—all of approximately equal height—established a rhythm and flow to the room while avoiding the roller coaster effect that was evident in the previous arrangement.

To achieve elegance, the country quilt on the club chair was replaced with a luxurious satin-stripe slipcover, and a matching ottoman was used in place of the more ordinary glass-top coffee table. The small Tiffany-style lamp, which detracted from the room's focal point, was replaced by a sleek pharmacy lamp, imported from the bedroom, placed next to the chaise.

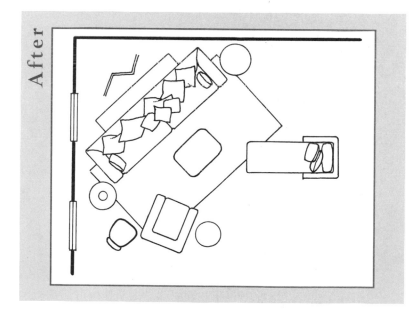

After

What We Banished

- Coffee table
- Wooden armchair
- Square wood side table
- Four-paneled wood screen
- Tiffany-style lamp
- Quilt
- Throw pillows

What We Borrowed

- Round wooden side table

- Pharmacy lamp

What We Bought

- Slipcover for chair
- Slipcovered ottoman
- Painted screen
- Two metal sconces
- Wheatback chair
- Metal and glass side table

Finding the Focal Point

Use What You Have:
Cherished Objects

Many of us have special treasures that we want to see displayed in our homes. There are lots of ways to adapt prized pieces, from the smallest precious vase to a grand piano, not only to show them off but to make them the focal points in our homes. Small pieces can be exhibited, museumlike, in clear Lucite boxes mounted on a pedestal or hung on the wall. Dramatic pinpoint lighting will further enhance the importance of the piece. Or a very fine object such as a large antique clock can be set up as the centerpiece with other complementary pieces. Even collections can be arranged to make them the focal point of a room, but this should always be done with an eye to creating a well-organized display. *Remember, whether you choose to use one object or a grouping, place it against the wall if you want to have an effective focal point.* (See chapter 9 for more about displaying accessories.)

If you own an antique piece, draw more attention to it by placing it on a spotlighted pedestal. The pedestal should be made of contrasting material. A

This collection of African carvings has been used effectively to enhance the simple mantel, creating a dramatic focal point that the fireplace, on its own, did not achieve.

An Ethiopian robe, hung in a simple Lucite box, is equally at home in a sleek minimal interior or a traditional setting.

wooden carving should not sit on a wooden base, for example. If your home decor is modern, use a pedestal of black lacquer or stainless steel. Marble or stained wood works best in a traditional setting.

A particularly delicate piece, such as Chinese porcelain, can be the center of a grouping of related pieces. The grouping then becomes a strong enough statement to make a focal point.

If you own a grand piano, no matter how grand it is, it is still a piece of furniture. I'd like to suggest that the only time it should be considered a focal point is in the home of a professional pianist, where all the furniture is grouped around it. In this case, it can still be decorated when not in use: a shawl or obi thrown over the top with a sterling silver candelabra or photos in silver frames can be used as accents. Remember to have the piano turned so that the pianist is facing the group, and if space is limited, keep the straight side of the piano against the wall.

A Home Fit for a King

The 21' x 18' living room of this Nashville home is a beautifully proportioned space with high ceilings, beams, and a graceful, simple fireplace. Three large windows with southern exposures provide lots of light, but the room was sparsely furnished, almost spartan, with the leather sofa pressed tightly under the window, two small glass tables on top of a sisal rug, and two black matching armless chairs (one is not visible) on the opposite wall. A tall, contemporary black metal lamp stood in-between the two chairs. Everything appeared to be adrift in the large space, including the small painting hanging high over the mantelpiece.

Everybody has a secret passion. In the case of this home-owner, it was her collection of Elvis books and memorabilia. What better way to create a focal point for this room than to highlight its most underutilized architectural feature, the fire-place, with pieces of a much-loved collection?

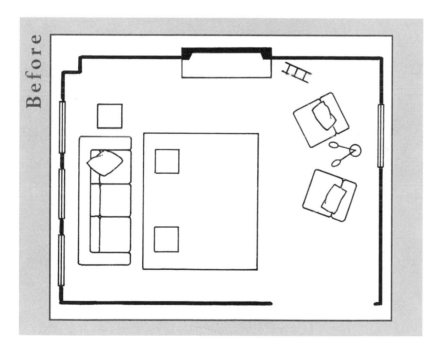

Before

Other Common Mistakes

- **Uncomfortable conversation area**

Clue: **Can we talk?**

- **Poor furniture placement**

Clue: **The furniture hugs the walls.**

- **Improper use of artwork**

Clue: **That little painting is drifting on the wall.**

- **Ineffective use of accessories**

Clue: **Do the small bits and pieces scattered ran-domly around the room enhance the space?**

- **Using lighting incorrectly**

Clue: **Even with two arms, is one lamp sufficient for the whole room?**

Finding the Focal Point

We arranged the sofa and two armless chairs in the middle of the room on the sisal rug to create a well-defined conversation area facing the fireplace. In the center of this new arrangement, the two glass tables were pulled together. A mate to the black metal standing lamp was brought in from the bedroom. One lamp was placed behind each chair to provide more light, to reinforce the focus on the fireplace, and to achieve a balanced look.

Finally, we gave the mantel even more impact by gathering framed posters (along with an Elvis magnet from the fridge) to compose a very special tribute to the King.

What We Banished

- **Nothing**

What We Borrowed

- **A standing lamp**
- **Framed artwork**
- **A fridge magnet**

What We Bought

- **Throw pillows**
- **A chenille throw**
- **Bone and black accessories for the coffee table**

Before

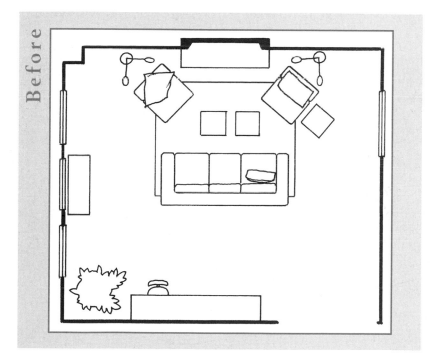

Focal Points in Other Rooms

In rooms other than the living room, the focal point is more often than not defined by the use of the room. The bed in the bedroom or a wall of books in a study are the most obvious examples. One important exception is found in the dining room, where the table or its decoration cannot serve as the room's centerpiece.

The Dining Room

The same guidelines that help establish the focal point in the living room apply to the dining room. Therefore, your dining table, with its central location, is automatically eliminated as a focal point. And it's not just placement that is a factor; even if your table is against a wall, it still won't qualify because there's nothing visually important on the wall. Remember, the focal point must dominate one *wall*. What will work? A buffet with a large painting, a grouping, or a framed mirror above it; an extremely large oil painting; or a mural alone on one wall. And of course, a fireplace with art hung above, a wall of sliding or French doors, or a large picture window will always dominate a room—

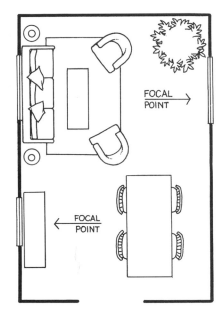

This combined living and dining room has two separate focal points—the large living room window at one end, and an oil painting hung above a server in the other.

any room—visually. If you choose to make your sideboard the focal point, you can use two dining chairs to flank it and make it more important.

If you have a combined living room and dining room—whether it's an L shape or long rectangle—each area needs its own focal point.

The large oil painting creates a strong focal point for this dining room and is reinforced by the Asian-style tableware.

The Bedroom

In the bedroom, the bed is almost always the focal point simply because of its size.

With the bed placed against the longest wall, you will want to follow the same guidelines that we discussed earlier for creating and enhancing a focal point. If you don't have a headboard, you can create an attractive backdrop with a decorative or metal screen or panel behind the bed. If you have a simple headboard, you may want to hang a wide painting or a trio of framed prints above the bed. An elaborate headboard will serve as a focal point with no additional enhancement necessary. Matching end tables with lamps will make the bed seem wider, giving it additional prominence as the focal point.

Many bedrooms do not have a long wall uninterrupted by doors and windows. You might consider positioning your bed in front of a double or large picture window. This will create a more dramatic focal point, especially if there is a good view. Also, you can accentuate the appeal of the bed itself by using linens and accessories to their best advantage. (See chapter 12 for more on how to make a bed.) Even if you have a large armoire or a dresser with a grand mirror, the bed and its headboard remain the only focal point with few exceptions, such as a wall of glass doors or windows that reveal a great view.

The Foyer

It can be dramatic or simple, fussy or serene—the focal point of your foyer has two jobs. It must attract you *and* welcome you. An ornately carved mirror above a bombé chest commands attention with its elegance. A large oil painting of a sunny seascape paired with a weathered pine bench please your eyes with their warmth. The image of an eye-catching framed black-and-white photo leaning on an ebony shelf in a tiny vestibule is difficult to ignore. And just as a travel brochure is meant to draw the traveler to more exciting destinations, an alluring focal point will make whoever walks through the door eager to see more.

Your Focal Point Checklist

To make sure that you have found or created an effective focal point, consider the following:

- Have you identified the largest, most dramatic element in your room?

- Does your conversation area face the focal point or is it part of it?

- Have you reinforced the focal point by placing other furnishings and accessories around it to balance and emphasize it?

- Is the painting, mirror, or screen over or behind the sofa both large and dramatic enough to provide the impact you want?

- If you are using a medium-sized armoire, bookcase, or wall unit as a focal point, are you using art or accessories on either side of it to make it look broader and more striking?

- Can you use a cherished keepsake or antique piece to create the focal point?

- Have you created a focal point for your dining room other than the table?

- If you have a combined living and dining room, have you balanced the focal points for each room so that they are distinctive yet do not overpower one another?

- Do accessories and art reinforce your bed as the focal point of the bedroom?

- Do you have a piece of art or a mirror above a shelf or chest in your entrance?

- Are you comfortable?

Chapter Eight

Using Artwork Effectively

Whenever I discuss artwork during my decorating seminars, I ask the attendees to stand. This is not a gesture of reverence to art, nor is it a break to stretch, rather it's the best way I know to introduce the most common mistake I see: hanging art too high on the wall.

Because most of my students, and most people in general, have been told to hang art at eye level, I ask them what "eye level" means. Naturally, everyone always laughs when they look around the room and see how much it differs from person to person. So, I'm going to tell you what I say to them: There is no such thing as "eye level." This common misconception about how to deal with artwork is just one of many that I'll address in this chapter.

Artwork comes in many forms, shapes, and sizes. But, for the purposes of setting guidelines for the most effective ways to display your art, I would like to discuss art that is hung.

Art on the Wall

Paintings, prints, tapestries, screens, mirrors—even some three-dimensional objects—should be hung to show the pieces off to their best advantage while keeping them in harmony with the rest of your room. Of course your home is not a museum that can, or should, be exclusively devoted to displaying art, so you have to make some important decisions when it comes to deciding how to integrate your own collection with the rest of your decor. Here follow some simple guidelines to help you do this properly.

Use What You Have and What You Like

If you're like most people, you have more "art" than you comfortably know what to do with. You've probably been collecting bits and pieces over the years, adding things to your walls as you go along. And now that you're a "Use What You Haver," you're taking this opportunity to spruce up your rooms by rearranging and perhaps painting and cleaning. Well, the time has come for you to sort out your artwork as well and look at what you've got and how you can use it most effectively. Physically removing the art from every wall *before* you start the transformation of your rooms not only will help you to place your furniture without distraction but will give you a very different perspective on the pieces of art themselves.

Your first step is to decide what you really want to keep—the sentimental favorites, the pieces that you really love. Room by room, decide what you want to use, what can be moved to other places, what can be stored (for use at another time), and what can be given away. Already, you are well on the way to solving the problems of overcrowding and using art ineffectively.

First Things First

In the living room, if you've arranged your sofa on the longest wall to create your conversation area, chances are you'll want to use the most significant and largest piece of art you have above the sofa. As a matter of proportion, a painting that is 4½' x 3' is ideal. (The minimum should be 3' x 2½') Alternatively, you may decide to place a grouping over the sofa. Whether it's two large pieces, three medium-sized pieces that are the same size and framed alike, or as many as six or seven smaller pieces, the overall outside dimensions should be the same as one large piece, that is, 4½' x 3'. (More about hanging groups later.)

Less Is More

Legendary fashion designer Coco Chanel advised women to always check themselves in a full-length mirror and to take off one piece of jewelry before leaving home. Artwork is like a fashion accessory for your room. Too much and the beauty of each piece is diluted.

If you have a lot of artwork, follow the example of art museums and galleries, and rotate your collection. You'll be surprised at your renewed appreciation of pieces you've had (and taken for granted) for years.

To Everything There Is a Season

Many people already change the look of their rooms seasonally with simple modifications of draperies, slipcovers, and rugs, so why not the artwork as well? The light and cheery watercolor that feels so right in the bright sunshine of a summer afternoon might give way to a striking black-and-white photograph of a snow-covered park for the winter. You will want your art to contribute to the overall feeling you are trying to achieve, whatever the season.

Establish an Art-free Zone

In every room, one wall should be free of art to give the eye a resting place, and to prevent you from being overwhelmed. The size of the wall is not important. But it's necessary to keep in mind that if you have a large window you're using as a focal point, then that window should be thought of like a piece of art—a piece of living art, if you would. (And if you have a room that serves two functions, such as a living/dining area or a living room/foyer, you can create a visual demarcation between the two by hanging art on part of the common wall and not on the other. Or, establish the two distinct spaces with an "art-free zone" of at least three feet in between.)

The Fine Art, and Science, of Hanging Art

How High Is Too High?

That old maxim about hanging art at eye level just doesn't work. I recommend that you begin by holding your art at the place on the wall where you *think* it should be—then *lower* it by three inches. Miraculously, you'll hit the spot where it should be hung. (I've tested this theory with hundreds of clients and it works!) By the way, if you're worried that you'll be hitting your head on a painting you've hung behind the sofa using this rule of thumb, don't be. How often do you hit your head against the blank wall now? Or if you're worried that a lamp might block a picture hung on the wall behind it, don't be concerned. When you are hanging a piece of art as the focal point in a room, all the other rules of furniture placement come into play. Remember, your home is not a museum in which each painting needs to be viewed fully unobstructed.

Giving Your Art Breathing Space

Whether you have one large piece or a unified group, surround your art with enough "white space" to show it off. This also means that you'll want to avoid hanging pieces on a wall that is too small. Any wall that is less than 36" wide should be art-free. (Short walls between or beside doors, windows, and archways are not good display spaces because they are generally too small to sustain the art.) If you are using a large window as a focal point in the room, you will want to keep the walls on either side of it blank for at least 36" from the edge of the woodwork of the window. Also, avoid hanging two pieces of art on adjacent walls at a corner. They will only compete with each other, and you won't be able to appreciate either.

Achieving Balance

The human eye seeks a straight line for balance. (If you've ever been seasick you know that the quickest way to make yourself feel better is to look at the horizon.) To give you, and your room, a calmer feeling, make sure that the bottoms of pieces that are hung together are flush with one another if they are nearly the same shape and size. If you are combining vertical pieces with horizontal pieces in a row, all of the vertical pieces should be hung with flush bottoms, and slightly higher; all of the horizontal pieces should hang with their bottoms at the same level.

This simple arrangement of art shows both horizontal and vertical pieces. In this case, the prints are further unified by style and size.

Group Dynamics

Whether you're working with two or a few pieces of art on one wall, there are some very simple rules to follow to make each piece in the group look good individually and together in your rooms:

- **Like with like:** Avoid mixing different mediums—oils, watercolors, drawings, photos, mirrors. The closer things are together in texture, color, and style, the more they will complement one another and make for a cohesive group.

- **Complementary frames:** Mixing different finishes together will cause the pieces to fight. Frames do not have to match, but choose the same material—gold or silver leaf, wood, lacquers, metal—so they look cohesive and don't distract from what is inside the frame.

- **Two of a kind:** Pairs of prints, drawings, or paintings are a value-added feature. Not only do they complement each other, they add balance and rhythm to a room. These matching pieces of art should be framed and matted identically and hung at the same level with their bottoms flush.

- **Arrange before you start to hammer:** There's an old axiom in carpentry, "Measure twice, cut once." It's a rule that saves lots of time and money. The same thing can be said for picture hanging. Before you pick up the hammer and nails, gather all of the pieces of art you're considering for a group and lay them out on the floor to test run your arrangement. (It's best to lay them out on a blank background—trying to decide on the best grouping against a patterned carpet, for instance, can be very distracting. If you don't have solid flooring, use a backdrop of a plain sheet or blanket.) There are no hard-and-fast rules about the distance between each piece but it's best to place them anywhere from 1½" to 3" apart within the grouping. You want them close enough to present a cohesive look but not so close that they crowd each other. Much depends on the size of the pieces. Also, take note of the overall dimension of the grouping to determine if it will fit the space you have in mind.

- **Hanging art on more than one wall:** It's best to limit artwork to two walls, if possible. If one wall has a large horizontal painting, try to use one or two vertical pieces on another wall for greater diversity. Do not be concerned about having the art on different walls be of consistent height. Just isolate each wall (as you learned in chapter 5) and hang each piece or grouping accordingly.

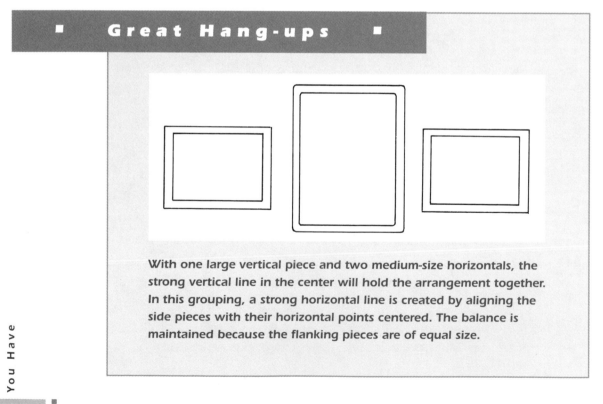

▪ Great Hang-ups ▪

With one large vertical piece and two medium-size horizontals, the strong vertical line in the center will hold the arrangement together. In this grouping, a strong horizontal line is created by aligning the side pieces with their horizontal points centered. The balance is maintained because the flanking pieces are of equal size.

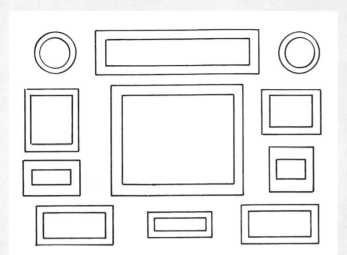

In this grouping of eleven pieces of varying sizes and shapes, the largest takes the central place with the others radiating from it in size position, from biggest to smallest.

When one horizontal piece is not wide enough, it needs to be balanced by two medium-size vertical pieces. Ideally, the bottoms should be flush.

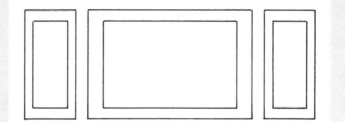

The arrangement of seven pieces of art of varying sizes avoids the roller-coaster effect by placing all the bottom pictures firmly flush. The rest of the wall, on both sides, should be "art free."

"Less Is More"

Before

The couple who owned this Dallas apartment used the dining area as a home office. Four different black-and-white pieces by the same artist covered the walls. Another piece was on a tabletop. There was just too much of a good thing. Also, pieces were hung on walls that were too narrow (that is, less than 36" wide) to show them off to their best advantage.

After

All four of the smaller pieces were stored away for six months, and only the large piece remained. Having the white space on the side walls allowed the large singular black-and-white to be appreciated without distraction. Half a year later, the larger piece would, in turn, be taken down, and the other black-and-whites, grouped together, would replace it.

About Frames

Once you've sorted all the artwork in your home—taken it off the walls, chosen what you *really* love and what you can live without, what will work seasonally and what pieces can be stored away for later use—your decisions about what to hang where will begin with the guidelines for selection and hanging we've already talked about. But because frames are so important to the individual piece of art, the groupings, and the look of the room overall, you should spend some time considering how the frames on your art work together, or don't. While it's likely that some of the pieces you already own will be compatible—since most of us tend to pick the same styles, even over many years—you'll probably decide that many of your pieces will look better in new frames. Here are a few rules that I've gleaned over the years working with a wide range of styles and tastes:

- Art hung in a grouping should all be framed in the same materials: natural wood, lacquer, gold or silver gilt, metal, or whatever.

- Framing styles and materials should complement both the individual piece and the room: botanical prints, realistic paintings, etc., in a traditional decor can carry gold or silver leaf, brass, ornate, or carved wood. Abstract or other modern pieces in a contemporary setting are compatible with metal—pewter, stainless, brass—wood, or lacquer in sleeker styles.

- The style of the frame can set the mood for the whole room: Highly polished, wooden frames with rounded corners are often paired with Asian prints. Rough-hewn timber frames set a country mood for native landscapes or portraits.

- Appropriate matting, in addition to framing, can add to the finished look of any piece of art, from prints to watercolors and oils to lithographs. From the vast range of fabrics, textures, and colors of matting materials—cotton, paper, silk—you will want to choose the one that's best suited to the art and the room's decor. While it's a common mistake to have matting that is too small, you do not want the matting, or the frame, to overwhelm a piece. (ReWard: Matting can also add considerable dimension to a favorite small piece, turning it into a dramatic focal point for your room.)

THE EASY WAY TO HANG A PICTURE ■

1. Determine where you want to hang the picture.

2. Hold the picture in one hand and place the index finger of the other hand at the center of the wire in the back, with the palm facing the wall.

3. Mark the place where the nail/hook will go by pressing your finger against the wall. The natural oils from your skin will leave a strong enough impression for you to follow (or you can put a small dab of toothpaste on your finger to mark the spot).

Note: You don't need to cover the spot with cellophane or masking tape before you hammer in the nail. It's a misconception that tape will prevent the plaster from cracking. It may, in fact, pull the plaster away from the wall or damage the paint.

I recommend using Ook brand picture hangers with the small, ridged, round-headed nails that come marked for pictures of various weights. They are the easiest to use and leave the smallest hole in the wall.

Birds of a Feather . . .

Before

Ashley and Nick's home in Des Moines had a macramé wall hanging, an oil painting, and drawings that were hung on adjacent walls in their living room. Because there were so many different mediums, nothing worked together.

After

After taking every piece of art down from the living room walls, we created a grouping of just drawings that were hung over the sofa for a more homogeneous arrangement. The big painting was moved to the entrance foyer, and the wall hanging was eliminated.

Using Artwork Effectively

About Mirrors

Mirrors, whether wall-to-wall or decoratively framed, can be both beautiful and functional if you use them wisely. Like other forms of on-the-wall art, mirrors can add touches of elegance and style to any room. But they are unique because they can enhance a room architecturally in a way that no painting, print, or wall hanging can do.

At one time, wall-to-wall mirroring in a variety of styles and colors—veined, beveled, or square tiles in bronze, coral, and gray—was being used in a primarily *decorative* way. As decoration, these patterned and colored mirrors were more distracting than attractive. Today, the main purpose of a wall of mirrors should be to expand a room visually.

The most effective type of mirror to add depth to a room is plain, clear glass. Situated where it will reflect a window and its view, a mirrored wall creates a second "window" in the room and increases the amount of light. (If you don't want to permanently install wall-to-wall mirror, you can hang or prop a very large mirror, framed or unframed, that will serve the same purpose.) However, one fully mirrored wall in a room does mean one less wall that's available for hanging art since you will still want to have at least one "art-free" wall in the room.

Wherever you use a mirror for architectural effect, the mirror itself should not be obvious. Attention should only be drawn to a mirror when it is contained within a beautiful frame or finished in a decorative style.

Framed or decorative mirrors present their own challenges and opportunities because they can be used as on-the-wall art, as architectural enhancements, *and* for the functional purpose of looking at yourself.

In a foyer, a large framed mirror, hung above a table or chest, can be the centerpiece of a focal point as well as being functional. A classic bull's-eye convex mirror or sunburst style can add lots of panache to a room. And for country-style interiors, those windowpane mirrors not only add to the overall look of the room, but they also can create the illusion of a real window on a windowless wall. But, as with any distinctive decorating element, avoid overusing them.

You will want to follow the same guidelines in hanging mirrors as for hanging art—not too high! But you also need to keep in mind the function of the mirror: there's nothing as frustrating as trying to use a mirror that cuts the top of your head off! So hang it at the right height for the room *and* for your own use.

The shape and size of the mirrors you use should also fit the space appropriately. Above a sofa, for instance, the mirror should be large and horizontal to offset the width of the furniture. If you use a round or square mirror, you will have to flank it with a pair of smaller pieces of art or a pair of sconces to give it balance and the proper proportion. (Be careful if you use multiple mirrors in a group because you could easily end up with a "fun-house" look.)

About Photographs

Whether they're family snapshots from your vacation, graduation or wedding portraits, or fine-art prints, photographs probably play an important part in your home. But not all photographs are "art" and each category needs to be treated in its own way.

Fine-art photographs, in black-and-white or color, should generally be treated just the way you do other pieces of hanging art. Since photos generally lend a casual feeling to a room, they are often best used in less formal areas or in a contemporary setting that complements the look of modern photography. In groupings, it's best to keep black-and-white and color separate unless the images are linked thematically. Framing and matting should be simple and complementary to the room's decor.

Black-and-white formal or professional photographic portraits can be gathered together in a family gallery. Mounted in large white mats and simple black frames, a collection of black-and-white photos becomes a dramatic focal point in a family room, hallway, or study. (I like to think of smaller casual snapshots as "accessories." In complementary frames, they are best displayed in groups on shelves or tabletops, but more about this in chapter 9.)

Art All Around the House

Every room in your home has a different look and so should the art that is hung there. In order to complement each space with hanging accents, it's important to distinguish what goes where and why.

In the Dining Room

As does the living room, the dining room requires more sophisticated art. Because diners are held captive at the table for long periods of time and their other senses are competing for attention, it's important to use artwork that will enhance the dining experience. Remember, your dining table can never be a focal point, so most likely the artwork will be the focus.

A thematic scheme such as a display of plates is appropriate. If you've carefully edited the art in your living room, chances are you'll have a few pieces left over that can be hung here. Check to see if you have one large painting or a set of botanical prints that will fit on the long wall over your server or perhaps two smaller lithographs or pen-and-ink drawings that can be used to flank a narrow hutch. The large round mirror that didn't work over your sofa will shine alone on an open dining room wall.

Whatever you choose, remember to apply the same rules for framing, placement, and hanging that you've read about in the beginning of this chapter.

Creating a Garden on the Wall

Before

The dining room of Jon and Marianne's Rhode Island home had a lone botanical print hanging high on the wall. On a hunch, I asked the couple if they happened to have any others. Guess what? There were five more stored away.

After

After collecting the family of botanical prints, we grouped them together on the wall in two rows of three each, all with flush bottoms. The unified grouping had six times the impact. (ReWard: The arrangement of copper pots on the Korean tansu chest and this dramatic grouping of prints created a vivid focal point for this dining area.)

Using Artwork Effectively

In the Bedroom

As discussed in the previous chapter, the bed, by virtue of its size and position on the longest or most prominent wall, is the focal point in this room. You may use artwork to enhance it: a wide painting or grouping, a mirror, or screen behind the bed can serve this purpose.

Bedroom art should be pretty and restful to look at. Perhaps you can use one of the pieces that were too delicate for the living room here. Or a grouping of black-and-white or color family photos that you didn't have space for in the living room can be arranged in a single row above, or in place of, the headboard. If your bedroom is very small, consider mirroring the entire wall behind the bed instead of hanging a framed piece. Not only will it make the room feel bigger, but it will also serve as art on the wall if it reflects windows or the beauty of a well-dressed bed.

In the Bathroom

There are usually only two places to hang art in this room: over the towel bar or behind the toilet. Since the art in the bathroom is likely to be one of the most attractive elements in the room, and it will receive the occupant's undivided attention, choose carefully. One piece is all you need. You might select something with a strong graphic impact such as a Japanese woodblock print or a black-and-white photograph. Or because the display space is probably limited, a small watercolor. Your framing materials should coordinate with the hardware or color scheme.

WALLPAPER ■

Coordinating art on walls that are hung with printed paper is like trying to mix different patterns in your clothing ensembles. It takes special attention to pull it off. For instance, a delicate floral still life can be overwhelmed by a flowered wallpaper. The bolder the pattern, the harder it may be to find complementary art. The best options are (a) a framed mirror or (b) simple monochromatic pieces such as lithographs. (Often artworks and wallpaper designs of the same period will have a natural affinity for each other. Have a look at photos of period homes where heavily patterned papers figure prominently and see how the artwork is handled in these authentic settings. For instance, a painting of darker hues and simple composition will stand up against a busy, patterned paper.) In any event, a deep simple matting or wide frame on any picture will provide "white space" around the work of art, separating it from the pattern of the paper. And you'll probably not want to hang large groupings on papered walls unless they are thematically related, such as a set of botanical prints.

Your Art Checklist

To make sure your art is being displayed most effectively, consider the following:

- Which pieces are most elegant to hang in your living room?

- Which pieces of art can be rotated seasonally?

- Which wall in each room will be art free?

- Are your pieces framed and hung with attention to creating a cohesive and balanced arrangement?

- Have photos been grouped to maximize their impact?

- Has your sculpture been displayed prominently?

- Are you using art in the room where it is most appropriate?

- Are you comfortable with your choices?

Chapter Nine

Skillfully Displaying Your Accessories

Have you ever walked into a room that had every surface covered with, as the English say, "bits and pieces"? Framed pictures, paperweights, and plants were crowded on tabletops in no particular order. The coffee table was awash with magazines, along with a candy dish or two, and a piece of colored glass. In the bookcase, more framed photos were crowded in front of hardcovers and paperbacks of all sizes, which were fighting for space with everything from figurines to candlesticks to a diploma encased in Lucite.

How did you feel in that room? Did it leave you feeling overwhelmed? Were you comfortable there?

Whether you call them bric-a-brac, tchotchkes, or objets d'art, your possessions speak volumes about who you are and what you like. They represent your unique style and what you cherish.

But I do understand the frustration in a client's voice when I hear, as I often do, "What should I do with all of my stuff?"

Your "stuff" can be overwhelming. So, the first thing you have to do is make sure that all of the other major aspects of decorating your room have been addressed before you tackle your accessories. It's just like dressing yourself: you normally don't pick a belt, necklace, or earrings before you choose the outfit you're going to wear. Follow the same general procedure and it will simplify the entire process.

Collections can be made up of various things, as long as there is one unifying element. In this case, we used the home-owner's collection of wooden objects on the coffee table. The small number of pieces chosen not only highlight each other, but leave enough free surface for the table's other functions—to serve, to put your feet up, to set things down.

The Three Secrets You Need to Know

To show off your "stuff" with the maximum impact, here are some of my secrets:

1 Three of a kind make a "collection."

Whether you have priceless Asian figurines or handmade wooden boxes, baseball caps, or snow globes, three or more of anything can make the beginnings of a collection. While a pair may help create balance, it doesn't create a strong enough statement to be called a "collection."

2 Gather like pieces together in one place.

Most of us are "collectors," whether by design or not. And chances are you'll find bits and pieces of related things all over the house that, when brought together, can suddenly command a lot of attention.

3 Rotate collections.

Art galleries and museums share the same problem with most people—they have too much to show properly at any one time. While they can loan stuff to other places, this is probably not the solution for you. But you can store several things and then bring them out for a change of scenery. Or, like your wardrobe, accessories in your home can be rotated seasonally.

Dealing with Your Stuff

I've learned a surefire technique for getting rid of clutter (and discovering gems) from a friend in the fashion trade. About once a year she takes everything out of her closets—and I mean everything. She discards or gives away anything that (a) doesn't fit, (b) she doesn't like anymore, or (c) she

The collection in this Santa Barbara home was created by gathering silver pieces of the same shape from all over the house. Pairing this round table with the round objects compounds the visual impact.

hasn't worn in more than a year. From what's left, she decides what she really needs—and loves—and these items get cleaned, repaired, and put back into the closet. The same strategy can be used to sort out all of your stuff:

Step 1 Make a clean sweep of all the "social" rooms—living room, dining room, foyer, family room, kitchen. Remove *everything* from the surfaces, including photographs. (You can deal with your books separately.) Chances are you've got stuff stored away. Unless it's strictly seasonal, like Christmas ornaments and decorations, put it all out.

Step 2   Put everything together on one large surface, such as the dining room table. (For many of us, we might have to clear a big space on the floor, too!)

Step 3   Take a long hard look at what you've got. Be critical. Ask yourself which pieces you still really need and which pieces you can't possibly give up—like family heirlooms or memorabilia—or, most important, which pieces you really love!

Step 4   Sort out what is left. Group similar things together—all vases, candles, photos, etc. (You'll immediately see the extent of your personal "collections.") Store seasonal items. Clean and repair anything that needs it.

Use What You Like and What You Have

On a recent consultation in St. Louis, I met a couple whose hobby was clearly music. Their living room was cluttered with five bulky guitar cases sitting on the floor. Inside each case, I discovered the most beautifully crafted instruments—these guitars were works of art. So we decided to display this collection by hanging all five on big brass hooks across the longest wall of the room. The guitars were still accessible for frequent use but they created a wonderful focal point for the room as well as an effective way for this couple to use what they had and loved.

No matter what you collect, it is an important and personal reflection of who you are. To display your possessions most effectively you will want to keep in mind the same principles that we used to hang art: give them the right space, in the right place. The following general guidelines apply to almost every item in your home. We'll address some specific items, including photographs and books separately.

I love Roseville pottery. Here's a collection in my own home. The pieces are displayed against a white background so that the colors appear to be more vibrant. When you gather the pieces of your collections together, you will experience an immediate and renewed appreciation for them.

First Things First

Once you have sorted out all of your collectibles, you will have to decide where they can be placed. If you have more than one kind of collection, keep them separated. Find the most suitable surfaces to mount your display. Side or end tables, coffee tables, shelves (open or closed) should be large enough to accommodate what you have without crowding. Let the theme of your collection suit the room: some items can be displayed in any room but others will find a natural environment in the kitchen, dining room, or den.

Less Is More

You may not be able to comfortably display all of your things at the same time. Trying to put too much—dozens of little figurines on a small side table, for instance—will only distract from the individual pieces. Give each grouping room to breathe. You can always rotate your collections seasonally or as the mood strikes you.

Establish a "Free Zone"

No matter how much stuff you have, you need to have some surfaces free of objects. I strongly recommend that windowsills be kept clutter free. With the exception of a very deep bay window, nothing adds to an untidy look as much as a hodgepodge on a windowsill. Even radiator covers that are built in to the sill should be left clear. You will want to refrain from placing several items on a small end table that already holds a large lamp. (We'll talk about coffee tables later in this section.) And if you are displaying a collection or group of accessories on your coffee table, consider leaving end tables accessory free.

The Fine Art, and Science, of Display

I've learned a few tips from the pros—the folks that mount those enticing displays in windows and stores. They have to work with as wide a range of goods as you're likely to have in your home, and they have to make these displays enticing enough to get us to part with our hard-earned money. Check out your favorite stores with this perspective in mind. Chances are you'll discover even more clever and attractive ways to show off your valued possessions:

Like with like: A collection is not only made up of thematically related items; it can also be comprised of similar materials such as

The Gallé glass that is displayed on this desk shows how impressive even a small collection can be.

silver, crystal, china, or wood. Don't mix materials unless you are going for a theme: dog figurines, birdhouses, miniature furniture, or angels. By showing similar materials together, you give the display a cohesive and impressive look. In a living room vitrine or a dining room breakfront, separate materials by shelf (i.e., silver on top, crystal in the middle, porcelain on the bottom).

Achieve balance: In a grouping of various sized pieces, set the largest one in the center, with the smaller pieces radiating around it in size order. On a shelf, the centerpiece should be the most impressive one (in most instances, the largest piece) with others in size order flanking it. Let pairs help you keep a balanced look. Even with only three pieces, a pair of things (such as candlesticks) flanking a larger object will make a striking impression.

Tallest in the back: When your class photograph was being taken, the tall children stood in the back, and the short ones in front. It's only logical that you'll want the best visibility for all your pieces, so arrange them from big to small just like the kids in that class photo. On the shelf of a dining room hutch, for example, silver trays can stand as a backdrop for the rest of your silver pieces—jugs, coffee or teapots, creamers and sugar bowls, salt and pepper shakers—all in descending size order in front.

Details: Sometimes it's the most subtle touches that can make a real difference. A line of teacups with all the handles facing out, left or right from the center teapot, has a sense of order and establishes an essential focal point. A crystal decanter can be centered on a dining room shelf with water, wine, and champagne glasses flanking it in descending order from largest in the center to smallest at the ends. Or a large bowl can be placed in the middle with smaller ones on the sides. You get the picture. It's always big in the middle down to smallest at the sides.

A Before-and-After Story:

The Hung-up
Dining Room

The dining room in the Lees' cozy Minneapolis house
held a large collection of decorative plates that were
scattered throughout the room. A decorative mirror was
hung horizontally above the serving piece but wasn't effec-

tively enhancing the area. On the same wall in the corner a not-very-attractive exposed air-conditioning unit really needed to be camouflaged. Aside from the less-than-optimal display of plates, the placement of the furniture needed to be dealt with first. The brightly covered dining table floated in total isolation in the middle of the room—"screaming distance" from the chairs that were pushed into the corners. The real function of this room was lost. It was clear that when it was time for dinner, a lot of lifting and moving had to be done to make this room work properly. Our challenge here was to correct a number of problems and thereby show off both the furnishings and the collection of plates to their best advantage. We needed to make the room both inviting *and* functional.

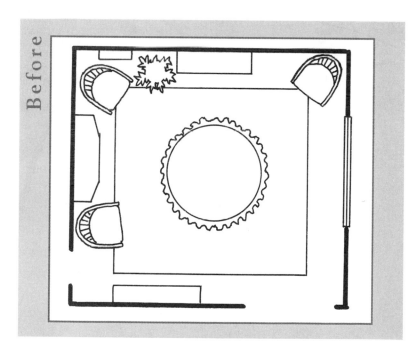

Before

Other Common Mistakes

- **An uncomfortable conversation area**

Clue: Could you have an intimate conversation sitting in this room?

- **Poor furniture placement**

Clue: Look for the wallflowers!

- **Ignoring the room's focal point**

Clue: Is any one element dramatic enough?

- **Furniture of different heights**

Clue: Can you trace the roller-coaster effect?

- **Improper use of artwork**

Clue: Is the mirror used to its best advantage?

Skillfully Displaying Your Accessories

The way we displayed the Lees' plates called to mind the deep decorative borders that were so popular in Victorian homes where the high walls allowed for such innovative decoration. The simple moldings made the perfect unifying element upon which the plates were "hung." This collection was showcased without the distractions of the other pieces on the wall. It turned out to be a wonderful way to display objects that were in keeping with the function of the room but without overwhelming it completely.

Even though the rearrangement of the plates is the primary lesson of this before-and-after, it was the attention paid to the rest of the room that allowed us to accomplish this transformation.

We removed the patterned cloth, which not only revealed a beautiful glass-topped bamboo pedestal table but also helped to move attention away from the busy fabric. (See chapter 7 for more on focal points.) The chairs were drawn up to the table to accommodate the room's natural conversation area and function. It also freed up the wall space, while still allowing traffic to flow around the room.

The mirror was rehung vertically above the server to balance the line of the tall hutch on the adjacent wall. We also

What We Banished

- **Flowered table-cloth**
- **Clock**
- **Miscellaneous accessories**

What We Borrowed

- **A candlestick lamp**

What We Bought

- **Nothing**

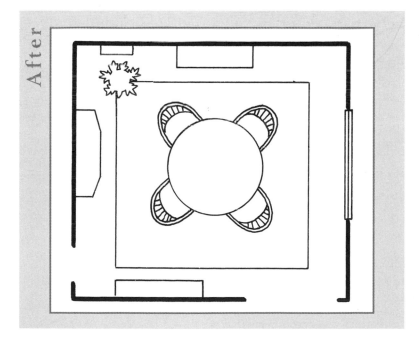

placed the tiny candlestick lamp and its mate from the living room on either end of the server with a vase of flowers, establishing a new focal point for the room. The leafy tree was moved to the corner to conceal the air-conditioning unit.

The room now had both the form and function which had eluded the Lees' previous arrangement. It allowed the beauty of their collection and the individual pieces of furniture to be shown off while escaping a "don't touch" museum feel.

About Photographs

Of all the accessories in your home, photographs are probably the most personal and treasured. Collections of photos tend to be organic— you're always adding new ones that celebrate important events in your life, places you've been, and sights you've seen. Personal photographs can also be a challenge to display since they come in many different sizes, shapes, and colors (or, to be more precise, color or black-and-white). In the previous chapter, we discussed photographs as art; here I offer you guidelines for using your photographs as accessories. To create the most attractive displays that will keep your photos from looking like a haphazard jumble, the following tips will be helpful:

Framing: Use one kind of framing material for all photos in a grouping—wood, steel, lacquer, brass, silver, copper, gold leaf—to bring a cohesive look to a number of images of different sizes, proportions, and colors. Choose frames that complement the decor of the room: silver adds a touch of elegance, polished wood is a handsome accent in a study or office, and lacquered frames are well suited to a contemporary look. (Personally, I'm not in favor of Lucite frames that don't lend anything to the photo or to the overall feel of the room. This is the one framing material that can *detract* from the elegance of any space.)

Instead of using an armoire to store china, here it is used to house a gallery of photos that have been arranged with the largest at the back—hung or propped up—for greatest visibility.

Tallest to smallest: Whether they're on a table or a shelf, arrange the largest photos at the back and the smallest ones in front. Photos, unlike many other collectibles, can sustain a little crowding.

One display per room: Determine where a grouping of photos will fit and place one grouping only in each room so as not to dilute their impact.

Rearview photos: Avoid displaying photos on a coffee table or other surface in the middle of the room since the backs will always be visible.

Photos with books: Photographs and books can coexist in a bookcase if you keep them well-organized, and on *separate* shelves. In a small, three- or four-shelf bookcase, arrange the books on the top and bottom with the photos in the middle. In larger or wall-to-wall units, arrange alternating bays with books and photos for a clean, librarylike look. (See the book section that follows.)

Black-and-white with color: Except for you purists, family photos in color or black-and-white can be grouped together on a tabletop. But there's a strong visual appeal in keeping old black-and-white or sepia-tone photos in one area and contemporary color photos in another.

About Books

Books are design accessories even as they enrich our lives in so many other ways. While the arrangement of your books can be dictated as much by the way you use your library as how it might look, cluttered bookshelves will detract from everything else in the room. Neatness does count. It not only makes the books look better, but it also makes your library easier to use. So, if you decide function overrides form on your bookshelf and you need to keep

The woman who owned this Washington, D.C., town house made the same mistakes that many others do. Books were covered by accessories and even some framed prints. The top of the bookcase was also used to display photographs and a tall vase, making the whole unit appear taller and even more out of balance with the rest of the room.

This is the same bookcase with all of the accessories, art, and photos removed. The books have been arranged by size and set flush to the edge of the shelves, resulting in a clean, dramatic, "library" look.

the books in alphabetical or category order, I offer five simple steps to make your library handsome and functional:

Step 1   Remove all the books from the shelves, making separate piles for hardcovers and paperbacks. (Take this opportunity to dust both the books and the shelves!)

Step 2   Unless you want your books in strict alphabetical or category order, arrange them by size, keeping hardcovers and paperbacks separate. (My preference is to have the hardcovers on the upper shelves and the paperbacks on the lower since hardcovers are generally more attractive and present a stronger display.) You can choose to arrange the books in two ways: (a) tallest to shortest from one side of the shelf to the other if you have one bookcase or (b) in two or more bays of books or bookcases, tallest to shortest from the middle outward.

Step 3:   Place every book with its spine flush to the edge of the shelf.

Step 4:   Refrain from adding anything except bookends or perhaps one or two simple accent pieces. Too many accessories combined with books will only detract from the clean line of your collection.

Step 5:   Keep the top of free-standing bookcases clear. Bits and pieces will add height to the shelf unit (which you probably don't need), and this clutter will undo the hard work you've put into reorganizing the books.

As with other accessories, I recommend that you try to keep all your books together in one room to display them most effectively. However, it's a good idea to keep a shelf of cookbooks handy in the kitchen and to use the occasional art or design book to accessorize other rooms.

About Plants

Plants, as photographs and books, are popular accessories. But, unless they are displayed properly, plants can distract more than they add to the decor of any room.

In the living room: This is the favored place for the indoor tree. I recommend the bamboo, Ming Aralia, and the long-leafed ficus. (For those who have had sad experiences with other varieties of ficus, take heart: The long-leafed variety is very hardy.) A tree not only adds living beauty to a room, but it can also serve many important functions. It can fill a vacant corner or balance a tall piece of furniture. Tall topiaries flanking a large window or glass doors can create a strong focal point for the room as it brings the outdoors inside.

Cement or stone planters can be used in any room and are ideal for great mounds of moss, English ivy, or other trailing plants. These plants can also be moved out-of-doors in the summer to be replaced by flowers, adding a seasonal burst of color to your room.

If you have more than one plant in a room, their containers should be complementary to each other and to the room. Terra-cotta pots, for instance, lend a southwestern or country air to a room. Brass will complement a traditional room. Stainless steel fits with a contemporary decor. Crackle-finished porcelain is elegant anywhere. (Spread moss over the top of the soil on all your potted plants to give them a finished look—it also helps hold in moisture in dry, centrally heated homes.)

Fresh flowers are a welcome addition to the living room at any time of the year. While the choice of varieties and colors is highly personal, arrangements made with several types of flowers in the same color are elegant and appropriate anywhere.

In the summer season, you can fill your fireplace with large green plants, flowering bushes, or dried arrangements.

This inviting Tudor-style home in New York State is made even more welcoming by the addition of fresh flowers and fruit. (Notice that only one kind of fruit is displayed as a color accent.)

In the kitchen: What better place to have a window box of fresh, fragrant herbs. (In fact, I recommend that a window box is the only thing that belongs on a sill!) Clay pots filled with ivy (real or silk) set on the top of your cabinets or on a high shelf add a touch of bright green. Professional garden designers always recommend using odd numbers of similar plants in a row, and I do also. I don't recommend hanging plants inside the house—they're such a throwback to the ubiquitous macramé plant holders of the 1970s. I suggest that we save hanging pots for the porch or veranda.

Pillow Talk

I love beautiful throw pillows. They are so versatile and useful in almost every room. They can add a touch of color to a plain sofa or turn a bed into an alluring lair. They can bring together different colors and fabrics to present a polished and luxurious look.

Most standard-sized sofas can accommodate four 18" square pillows. The basic arrangement calls for two in the back, points up, and two in front sitting squarely. The front pillows can match the sofa fabric, the back ones should contrast in an accent color or pick up the fabric from another chair (or even the dining room chair fabric in a living/dining room combination).

On a loveseat, place two pillows at the middle seam: the back one in an accent color, point up, and the front in the loveseat fabric squared off.

As long as the pillows make for a balanced arrangement on the sofa, you can now "layer" with an interesting contrasting shape: a bowling-ball size or triangular shape. Small, rectangular hand-embroidered accent or decorated pillows also work well.

Any throw pillow can be trimmed, with tassels, fringe (bullion or short), or self-welting, depending on the style of the sofa and the room. Pillows can also be slipcovered to change seasonally along with the rest of the room. Consider using velvet in the winter and raw silk or cotton slipcovers in the summer. On your bed, two European square pillows can be used in place of a headboard, and a long bolster can be propped behind standard pillows for a more sophisticated look.

Pillows with their points up draw the eye upward to lighten
the effect of the heavy furniture.

About Candles

Candles are so reasonably priced and come in such a multitude of colors, scents, and styles that it's easy to understand why they are more popular than ever.

There are many ways to use candles decoratively. Thick beeswax candles can be arranged on the coffee table in a group, using three different sizes (it counts as one accent piece). Also, candles lend themselves to each season. Always keep the colors consistent throughout a room, and change them when you rotate your art and accessories. For instance, use all red or all green at Christmas, all marigold or bronze in the fall, all pale aqua or pale pink in the summer—depending on the colors in your room. White and ecru are classics that work all year long.

Note: Scented candles add an extra sensual element to a room. Don't,

HARDWARE ■

Everywhere throughout your home are the silent accessories: doorknobs, handles, pulls, electrical plates, hinges, hooks, etc. For the most part, these things are functional and should be "invisible." But many of these—doorknobs, pulls, and handles—are always in sight and can enhance, or detract, significantly from any room. Start with what you have. If your fixtures are chrome, you'll want to use that metal throughout the rest of the room. Since it's not always practical to modify metal finishes with paint, you could instead choose to change things selectively since there's such a wide range of choices available in every price range: brass, steel, lacquer. Many pulls and knobs are available in glass, wood, or ceramic. The simple change of pulls on a door or chest can add that finishing touch you've been looking for.

however, use them in a dining room or kitchen unless you have finished your meal. Their scent can detract from the taste of food.

About Open Storage: CD Holders and Wine Racks

CD holders, wine racks, and other "visible" storage units can clutter up a room. While there might be a place for a tall, free-standing CD rack in the den or a family room, they should be stored out of sight in the living room, which is always the most formal room in the house. Wine racks and other storage units should be kept in the rooms for which they are most appropriate—kitchen, bath, or bedroom.

About Bowls

A beautiful bowl filled with fruit can really give a room a big punch of color. And it is so versatile because you can change the look and selection seasonally. Bright green Granny Smith apples are a harbinger of spring, pomegranates define winter, lemons or limes are immediately identified with summer (prick them to add scent, too), and a bowl brimming with vivid persimmons bring the vibrancy of the fall harvest inside.

A word about glass bowls: Be careful when setting a clear glass bowl on a glass surface. The effect you're aiming for will be washed out. Instead, use contrasting materials.

About Clocks

Unless you have a collection of antique clocks or watches, you need only one timepiece per room. In the living room, you can place one on a mantel or center it on a shelf of your living room wall unit. Bedrooms often have clock radios or alarm clocks, and kitchens need only one large wall clock. And remember, if a clock hangs on the wall, all of the rules for hanging art apply. Don't hang it high over the door!

Your Accessories Checklist

To give your accessories maximum impact, consider the following:

- Have you gathered all accessories and put them together on your dining table?

- Have you organized your accessories and scattered collections after eliminating what you no longer need or want?

- Have you chosen complementary framing materials for your photographs?

- Have you reorganized your bookshelves?

- Are all plants in containers of the same material?

- Have you used throw pillows to accent your rooms?

- Is all the hardware in the room of the same finish?

- Are you using candles effectively?

- Are the collections you've created and the placement of your accessories making you feel more comfortable?

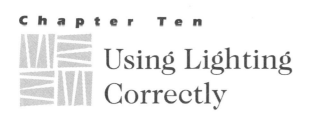

Chapter Ten

Using Lighting Correctly

Now that your furniture has been arranged for optimal beauty and comfort and your cherished art and accessories are being effectively displayed, at last, your home is ready for the one element that will really make it come to life: good lighting. Just as theatrical lighting affects the mood and tone of the set of a play, lighting your home well is critical to how well your home looks and functions.

I bet you've been to a number of homes where the furnishings were lovely and the space was well appointed, but everything was dark. Or you may remember homes that had lots of globe-style ceiling fixtures, but no matter how many lights were turned on, the rooms always seemed shadowy and dim.

Trying to read in one of these rooms was a real challenge. So you probably had to sit close by a window where, at least, you had natural light. However, if it was an overcast day, a winter afternoon, or evening, you were out of luck.

Perhaps the ceiling lights were covered by old-fashioned flat glass plates whose main purpose was only to conceal the bulbs. They certainly didn't enhance the room or the effectiveness of the lighting. If anything, all they did was force the light up to the ceiling, casting shadows on the room and people below.

Directing light upward had been a function of the old-fashioned incandescent torchère, too. One tall, thin lamp with one or two bulbs usually stood in a corner, and in most cases was more decorative than functional. The problem was that most people relied on it to light an entire room.

And then there was the greatly admired chandelier that hung over the dining room table. It had crystals galore, but the clear glass bulbs produced a harsh, glaring light throwing shadows on everyone and everything below.

Today, improper or inadequate lighting is still way up near the top of the list of the most common design mistakes people make. Everyday, I see stunning table lamps with the wrong bulbs or outdated overhead fixtures. Lighting can make or break a room, so it's not a surprise that almost all of my clients tell me that trying to light a room properly totally confuses them. If you, too, feel confused and overwhelmed by the prospect of determining what kind of lighting is appropriate for your needs, I'm recommending what you can—and can't—use so you won't ever be in the dark again about how to light your home correctly.

Lighting Options

Do you have a single ceiling fixture as the primary light source in any room? Does it have incandescent bulbs? Does the light beam up toward the ceiling instead of down on the room? Is the room filled with shadows? Does your room lack a well-lit place to read or work? Are your art and collections, as well as plants and trees, hidden in the dark?

If you have answered yes to any of these questions, it's time to figure out how to use what you have or upgrade to what you need. You probably already have some—or perhaps a lot—of what you need, but if you have to update and add to what is already there, chances are you'll be able to do this quickly and inexpensively.

To light your home properly, you need three types of lighting: general, task, and accent.

General Lighting

As the name implies, general lighting illuminates the room overall. This category includes any fixture that hangs on or near the ceiling. Torchères, which stand on the floor, are also included in this group because their light shines up.

Track Lighting

Track lighting is one type of general lighting. Unobtrusive and clean-looking, thin tracks are available in 4' and 8' lengths, in either white or black (for more contemporary interiors). Their long-lasting halogen spots provide excellent bright, white light that is flexible and can effectively replace standard ceiling fixtures that have incandescent bulbs. (One of my favorites is the PAR-3 from Lightolier; see Sources.)

If you already own track lighting with bulky-looking cans (that make the ceiling appear lower than it

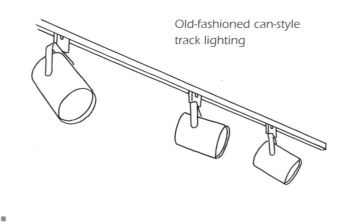

Old-fashioned can-style track lighting

actually is), keep the tracks and replace the cans with new tiny halogens. They will make your room look fresher, and because they are more energy efficient, they'll save you money.

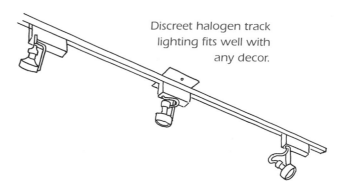

Discreet halogen track lighting fits well with any decor.

Advantages

- Tracks are multipurpose. They are adjustable and can illuminate furniture, art, and accessories as well as workplaces.
- Track can be used in every room in the house and it works well with all design styles.
- Small halogen track lights are unobtrusive.
- If you move, track lighting can be reused and reconfigured in your new home.

Disadvantages

- None

Recessed Lighting

Recessed lighting is usually found in newer or remodeled homes. And because it is built-in, it creates the illusion of higher ceilings since nothing is suspended from the ceiling.

Recessed lighting comes with interior baffles, which are metal linings of chrome, brass, white, or black metal. I always opt for the black metal baffles, which, unlike other choices, reduce glare.

If your home already has recessed lighting with the old, larger floodlights, replace them with smaller halogen high hats, which are less conspicuous and use less electricity.

Advantages

- Excellent light source
- Compatible with all styles of furniture
- Gives the impression of a higher ceiling with a clean look
- Unobtrusive

Disadvantages

- A permanent fixture that cannot be taken to a new home

Cove Lighting

Cove lighting is ideal if you have deep moldings running around the periphery of your rooms at ceiling level (or would like to add them). This treatment will showcase the architectural details and fine plaster work with general illumination. It is not usually strong enough to provide sufficient lighting for a whole room on its own.

Advantages

- Distinctive lighting that can add drama to a room

Disadvantages

- Only for homes with interesting ceiling detail that deserves to be highlighted
- Does not give the bright light that recessed or track lighting provides

Chandeliers

Chandeliers are a great favorite for use as a general light source, and it's easy to understand why. They're available in a multitude of styles, from simple brass to opulent crystal, and they can add lots of style to a room. Unfortunately, many chandeliers are not very effective when it comes to lighting a room because they illuminate only the ceiling directly above them. To correct the problem, use clip-on mini-shades to cover bulbs so that the fixture doesn't cast wild shadows on both the ceiling and the rest of the room below. And remember, clear bulbs should always be replaced with frosted bulbs to help eliminate glare.

Try the small, clip-on shades that are approximately 4" in diameter and are slightly wider at the bottom than the top. Use either smooth or gathered shades, not pleated. In addition to silk, the options include shiny craft or parchment paper, which work well with contemporary and country styles, and linen, which is compatible with all design styles. Basic colors range from white through parchment, and custom shades can be made in an infinite variety of styles, sizes, and colors. My personal favorite is the more dramatic angled "coolie hat"–shaped shade in any color or material. When you shop, take a light bulb with you to make sure that the shade fits on it properly.

The light from unshaded chandeliers can be harsh and can throw lots of unwanted shadows.

Small shades make a practical and stylish addition to most chandeliers.

Advantages

- An eye-catching fixture that can add a note of elegance
- Available in a wide range of styles, finishes, and prices
- Can be removed and taken to a new home

Disadvantages

- Casts shadows and glare if frosted bulbs and clip-on shades are not used

Torchères

Torchères are standing lamps that come in an assortment of styles and metals and beam light upward. Generally used for overall illumination, these lamps aren't necessarily very good for reading unless they have an added arm with a downlight. If you don't have a perfectly plastered and painted ceiling, you shouldn't consider torchères; they'll only highlight every crack and flaw. If you have overhead downlighting they're unnecessary. However, if you need ceiling lighting and your ceilings are flawless, then a pair of torchères will work for you. Be sure to place them either diagonally across the room from each other or have them flank your sofa or conversation area.

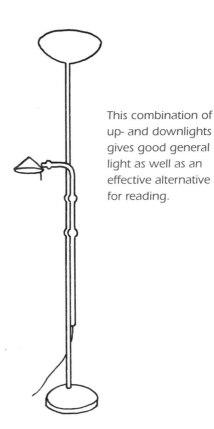

This combination of up- and downlights gives good general light as well as an effective alternative for reading.

Advantages

- A pair of torchères will provide good light and add elegance and symmetry.
- They can be moved from one room, or home, to another.

Disadvantages

- One is not sufficient as a general light source.
- They're appropriate only for rooms with unflawed ceilings.

Sconces

If you have sconces, or want to add them, make sure your walls are in very good condition. Just as torchères expose the ceiling, sconces highlight flaws on the walls.

Most traditional sconces have two candelabra-type arms in brass, crystal, or silver; contemporary sconces come in dozens of styles and are made of stone, glass, or metal. Some sconces have both up- and downlights with only a covering in the center. If your existing sconces need shades to rid the room of shadows, buy the same clip-on types used for chandeliers. If you have a chandelier and sconces in the same room, the shades should match or be coordinated.

A standard torchère provides good general illumination, but it will highlight any imperfection in the ceiling.

A traditional sconce with shades

Advantages

- Can be moved from home to home
- Available in a wide range of styles and prices
- Will add symmetry and elegance

Disadvantages

- Not an adequate light source by themselves
- May require through-the-wall wiring

Task Lighting

Task lighting—table or standing lamps, strip lighting, or track lighting directed to specific areas—is an essential element for working or reading comfortably. It offers more flexibility than general illumination because it is smaller and can be moved. But remember that it can not replace general lighting or you'll wind up with pools of light in a dark space.

Table lamps come in a wide variety of styles and sizes; some provide pools of light (such as the usual lamps found on end tables) and some give directed light (such as clamp or banker's lamps).

Table lamp for task lighting

Wall-mounted swing-arm lamps, with their wide range of motion, make ideal bedside lamps. They provide the same kind of illumination as a table lamp but don't take up valuable space on a side or end table. They come in an assortment of metal finishes that can be coordinated with your bedroom hardware.

Standing, or pharmacy, lamps—unlike torchères—cast light down. (Remember, if you use table or standing lamps, make sure you have a matching pair.)

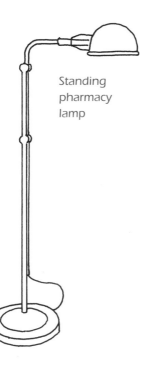

Standing pharmacy lamp

Advantages

- Essential for specific work areas—desk or countertops—and for reading
- Available in a wide variety of styles and price ranges
- Can be moved to different rooms and homes
- An easy way to add pairs, which create balance and cohesion

Disadvantages

- None

A versatile
swing-arm lamp

Accent Lighting

The third type of illumination your home requires is used to highlight paintings, collections, sculpture, trees, and plants. Properly lit artwork and important accessories can dramatically improve the look of these pieces and the overall feel of the room.

Beyond the traditional brass painting lights, there are accent lights available in a variety of metals and colors, including black, brushed brass, copper, chrome, and pewter in both contemporary and traditional styles. They are fashioned into a wide assortment of styles, from wide to pencil thin, to coordinate with the frame and decor of your room.

Adjustable, overhead, recessed, or track spotlights can be used to highlight a piece of sculpture or a centerpiece on a dining room table. While this is perhaps the most common method of illumination, you can also place your art on a pedestal with built-in lighting on the top surface.

Collections displayed in bookcases or wall units can be illuminated with individual mini-halogen spotlights or strip lighting under the shelf. (Collections are covered in chapter 9.)

IF YOU DON'T HAVE A VIEW, PLACE STRIP LIGHTING OR MINI-SPOTLIGHTS IN THE WINDOW BEHIND YOUR VALANCE.

EITHER WILL PROVIDE AN ACCENT DOWNLIGHT AND WILL MAKE A LESS-THAN-INTERESTING WINDOW MORE EYE-CATCHING AT NIGHT.

Until recently, cylindrical metal canisters, sitting right on the floor, were used to uplight a tree or a group of floor plants. Today, there are better, less conspicuous alternatives, including stake uplights (see Sources for Frontgate® Catalog). Two black metal stakes with tiny halogen lights on top are made to sink down into the soil. When they are inserted into the earth, the light comes up from the base of the tree, reflecting the pattern of the leaves on the ceiling. (Make sure the plant is light-worthy.)

Advantages

- Showcases prized art and accessories
- Can be moved from home to home

Disadvantages

- None

ReWard

If you own two lamps that are similar in size and height, just put identical shades on both to tie them together. If one is slightly lower than the other, place a painted wooden base or a small marble pedestal underneath the shorter one. This will raise the lamp up, making it seem taller than it really is, and reinforce the appearance of a pair.

In the Living Room

IF MESSY WIRES ARE DRIVING YOU CRAZY, USE A CORD-CONTROL KIT (AVAILABLE FROM THE HOLD EVERYTHING CATALOG; SEE SOURCES) TO CONCEAL THEM. CORD COVERS ARE AVAILABLE IN BLACK OR WHITE. A SINGLE WIRE CAN BE TAPED TO THE BACK OR UNDERSIDE OF A PIECE OF FURNITURE THAT IS AGAINST A WALL.

Almost everyone has problems properly lighting their living room because it requires a variety of light sources. It's surprising how many people complain that they don't have enough light; yet when I check their lamps, I almost always find the same easy-to-correct problem: they're not using the correct wattage for their lamps! Use the maximum wattage—up to 100 or 150 watts if possible—and be sure that three-way bulbs are in every three-way socket.

While end tables and table lamps are still popular, there are many other options available. Standing floor lamps, such as the pharmacy style, are available in a variety of metals, and have adjustable-height downlights. A pair of these, flanking a sofa, are great for reading and watching television. The best models will feature dimmers.

If you are using table lamps on end tables, remember that living room table lamps should measure between 26" and 30" high, depending on the height of your end table. In other words, if you have a low table, compensate with a slightly higher lamp, and vice versa.

FOR

SAFETY'S

SAKE, BE

SURE THAT

ANY

FABRICS,

SUCH AS

CURTAINS,

DO NOT

COME IN

CONTACT

WITH

HALOGEN

LIGHTS, AS

THE BULBS

BECOME

QUITE HOT.

Of course, when using table lamps it's best to have a pair, and my personal preference is that they match exactly. (I've observed that in many homes people own a matching pair of lamps, but one is in the living room and the other in the bedroom. Keep pairs together!)

Whichever type of table lamp you use, be sure that the lamp is *centered* in the middle when placed on an end table, and not pushed back, hugging the wall. It's more important to have accessible light and a balanced-looking table than it is to hide a few inches of wire.

Lamps need shades, and here again, there are a lot of choices. The fastest and simplest way to quickly update the look of your existing lamps is to purchase new shades. As is the case with clothes, lamp shade styles go in and out of fashion. Pleated shades have become outdated and, unless you have a 1950s-style home, very tall barrel-shaped lamp shades are considered passé.

The short, wide, barrel-shaped shades are classic, and shirred or gathered lamp shades are still a staple in traditional homes. And, of course, custom-made shades, with a variety of trims, are always an option. White, ivory, or

Lamp shades: gathered, coolie-shaped, and pleated

black are elegant in linen, paper, or silk. Brass, chrome, or pewter shades add drama to contemporary metal bases.

The most popular style being used now is the "coolie hat"–shaped shade that I mentioned earlier when we were talking about chandeliers. These shades are effective because they provide an angled counterpoint to all of the boxy lines in a room. Because of the wide bottom, the light underneath is spread out on all sides. They can be found in the same materials as the aforementioned clip-on shades: silk, craft paper, parchment or shiny paper, and linen.

DIMMERS, OUTLETS, AND SWITCHPLATES ■

When you install new lighting fixtures, the hardware should be as inconspicuous as possible. If you try to use them as decorative accents they become distractions.

Switchplates and electrical outlets should be painted or wallpapered, the same as the rest of the wall so that they blend in. Why spend money on an expensive brass outlet cover if you're just drawing attention to a plug? (If you own your home and your floor or table lighting is in the middle of the room, think about having an electrician install a couple of outlets directly in the floor below your lamps.)

Whether you own or rent your home, make sure that all the overhead fixtures have dimmers. Lutron makes some of the best dimmers around (see Sources). They are aesthetically pleasing, quiet, and you can take them with you when you move.

Banker's lamp

Architect's lamp

An updated
version of the
traditional
gooseneck
lamp equipped
with mini-
halogen bulbs

Remember: When you are shopping for a new shade, take your lamp with you!

If you have a work station set up in an armoire or wall unit, built-in strip lighting is a necessity. Placed into the area above a computer or desk, it will provide ample light. If you work at home there are other options as well:

- *A flexible, metal, architect's lamp (available in several finishes)*
- *A banker's lamp, the classic green-shaded, brass-based incandescent light*
- *A mini-halogen, generally available in a variety of styles and finishes*

In the Bedroom

Most bedrooms come with overhead fixtures but generally they don't provide sufficient light. The bedroom is traditionally the place for the more delicate-style standard lamps, which are commonly 22" to 28" high. (Any bigger and they'll be too large for most bedside tables.)

But the most practical and functional lighting fixtures for a bedroom are swing-arm lamps mounted on either side of the bed. These hinged, adjustable lamps are great for people who like to read in bed because they pivot to direct light where it is needed. Centered over each bedside table, they also free up the table for necessities like clock radios and telephones. I recommend using linen or silk "coolie hat" shades—you can tell I *really* like this style of shade—with a unit that has a three-way bulb capacity.

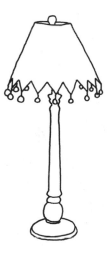

An alternative to the standard or swing-arm lamp is the metal clip-on or clamp light. Available at art or photo supply houses as well as lighting stores, these inexpensive workhorses work well with metal headboards in a contemporary interior. And for you minimalists who want a simple fixture, check out the tilting-head lamps sold at all lighting stores. Standing only 20" high, they allow you to direct light where you want it, but they generally will take only a 60-watt bulb.

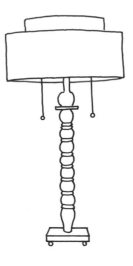

In the Kitchen

Kitchens may come with a standard overhead globe or fluorescent lighting fixture that can easily be changed to several recessed high hats (if you own the space) or one 4' or 8' length of track lighting. If you have an island in your kitchen, a separate track with suspended mini-halogens with white or colored glass shades will spotlight the work area. This eliminates the need to always turn on the overhead (general) lighting.

Strip lighting can be added under cabinets and offers good, direct light for your counter workspace. These low lights will change the ambiance of the room, too. And, as you know by know, flexibility means good design.

CFLS ■

Compact fluorescent light bulbs (CFLs) provide greater energy efficiency, but they cost a lot more than incandescent bulbs (roughly twenty dollars versus one dollar, respectively). However, the savings after several years of use are considerable—the CFL uses roughly one quarter less electricity than the incandescent. Standard compact fluorescents are a bit harsher than incandescents, so choose CFLs that are dimmable for rooms that need softer light.

In the Bathroom

If you have a medicine chest with strip lighting above it, you can make a quick, interesting change that will give the room a fresh look. Depending on the size of the sockets, you can use candelabra bulbs with squared-off sides (those long-tapered ones) or any unusual shape, alternating with the usual round bulbs for a postmodern look. Or, you can use all of one or another, as your mood dictates. By simply changing from round to more unusual-shaped bulbs, you will get a few different looks for just a few dollars. Try other combinations but, whatever you choose, remember to use frosted bulbs.

Your Lighting Checklist

To give your rooms the light they need, ask yourself if you have done the following:

- Identified all the places where general, task, or accent lighting is needed?
- Replaced flat overhead glass plates or globe fixtures with recessed, track, or chandelier lighting?
- Eliminated "big can" track lighting and replaced it with tiny, energy-saving halogen spots?
- Made sure that all recessed lighting has a black baffle or lining?
- Changed outdated floodlights in recessed lighting to halogen high hats?
- Changed all bulbs in lamps to maximum wattage?
- Used three-way bulbs in three-way sockets?
- Made sure that the height of lamps used together is equal?
- Made yourself more comfortable?

Part Two

Making Your Home Even More Beautiful

The Shell

At the beginning of this book, and at the start of every consultation, I ask this question: do you rent or do you own?

If you own your house or apartment, everything you do to it will ultimately affect its resale value—whenever that happens. I stress that it's important not only that you enjoy the changes you make but that these changes won't have a negative effect on prospective buyers. (If you want to have a purple kitchen, that's your choice. However, a potential buyer may walk in, take one look, and walk out because she can't get past the wall color to see the rest of the house and doesn't want to go through the hassle of redoing it.) Potential buyers are more concerned with what's already there than with what they might have to do.

For renters, the question of how long you plan to stay is no less crucial. Often, people who rent feel that they don't want to invest in a temporary home solely for the landlord's benefit. If you rent, I recommend changing only those things that will make you more comfortable immediately, and this usually means that the changes you make—the things you buy—will be those you can take with you when you leave.

Stripped of all the furnishing, art, and accessories, what remains in the room is what I call the shell—walls, floors, and windows. The issues that then need to be addressed are these: paint and wall covering, flooring, and window treatments. These components make up the basic setting or backdrop against which you will decorate your home. It doesn't matter how beautiful your furniture is, if the setting isn't in good shape, your home can't reach its full po-

tential. It's like putting on new, clean clothes without taking a shower first. No matter how attractive the clothing is, something is going to detract from it—in a big way.

Take a look at the walls in your home. Is the paint still in good condition or are there cracks in the ceiling or on the walls? What about the floors? Are the wood floors dirty and dull, or if you have carpeting or rugs, are they faded and worn? What about the window treatments? Do they enhance or detract?

When you work on the shell, remember to work, literally, from high to low. That means start with the ceiling first, then the walls and the windows, and finally the flooring.

Paint and Wall Coverings

If you rent your home and it's time to paint, buy the best quality you can afford. Even if your landlord is responsible for hiring and paying the painters you should provide the paint. It will make a big difference.

Finishes

Today, there are many types of paint, which give you a lot of options that go well beyond simply rolling on a coat of flat white. But to start with the standards, there are four basic paint finishes that we use for residential interiors:

Flat, which has virtually no shine to the finish, is the one for you if you don't have small children or a lot of traffic in your home. It is generally easy to apply and the flat finish does not accentuate any flaws on the surface, which makes it ideal for ceilings. The drawback is that you cannot clean flat painted walls easily.

Eggshell has a slight sheen and is well-suited for walls that need frequent wipe-ups. The surface to be painted needs to be in pretty good condition to take an eggshell finish well or it will call attention to imperfections.

Semi-gloss should be the paint of choice for all trim—doors and window frames, stair risers, baseboards—no matter what other paints you use on your walls. Kitchens and bathrooms should be painted entirely with semi-gloss or, at least, eggshell finish.

High gloss is usually reserved for trim and rarely used for walls because it shows every imperfection. If you're doing the work yourself, you'll probably want to stick with the other finishes.

Color

For most people, white is the safest choice. It is neutral and will save you the anxiety of choosing from the hundreds of colors that are available. But even with white, there is a wide range of hues. Because white is based on the three primary colors—red, yellow, and blue—the difference from one mix, finish, or brand to another can be dramatic.

To help you make the best choice of "white," follow this simple tip: if you don't have fabric swatches, carpet, or wood samples that you can carry around, go to your local paint store and select a variety of white paint chips that you *think* reflect the dominant colors in your rooms. When you bring the chips home, pick out the chip that is actually the right white paint color that will tie together everything you have. In addition, select one chip that is actually the same color as your fabric, one that matches your rug, etc. Even if you do have swatches, the paints chips are easier to carry with you, so you'll always have a ready color reference for an unexpected shopping trip.

You'll find that one or more hues are prevalent—blues, golds, pinks—and you'll want to select the white that best complements your furnishings. You'll also find that the range of whites can have an impact on the feel of the room: blue-whites will be clean and cool; pink/rose-whites will glow; and gold-tone whites will be warm. Here are a few basic guidelines about paint color.

Changing colors from room to room is determined by the style and floor plan of your home. Many contemporary houses and postwar apartments have open plans with rooms that flow from one to another without the demarcation of walls and doorways. Ideally, these homes should have one wall color throughout the entire space to avoid any awkward delineation. Conversely, traditional older homes and prewar apartments that have distinctly separated rooms can have a varied color scheme.

Contrasting colors for walls and trim is a commonly used technique that looks great if your room has a lot of unbroken wall space or beautiful moldings to be highlighted. But, if it has a lot of windows or more than two doors (including closet doors), stick with one paint color or it will accentuate architectural flaws and make the room feel smaller. If you're thinking of using a different color on your ceiling, consider the height of the room. High ceilings, at least nine feet tall, are generally better suited to deeper colors than standard height ceilings. Enveloping a room—walls and ceiling—in the same shade of white will make it feel bigger.

Ever popular beige, the darling of decorators in the late twentieth century, continues to be in vogue thanks to a broad spectrum of easy-to-take neutrals from ivory to taupe. Always elegant, this sophisticated palette complements a wide range of decorating styles and is an alternative to white for a light look.

Beyond Paint

Glazing, sponging, and marbleizing are effective ways to add interest to your walls and have become more popular with ready-made kits. But, like all good things, be careful not to use them too much or you'll end up with an overdecorated look. Keep an easy visual flow from room to room throughout the house.

If you have a small budget, stamping or stenciling kits offer an inexpensive decorative treatment. You can imprint a small, medium, or large border around a child's bedroom, a hallway, or a bathroom. Again, like all decorative elements, you'll want to use these techniques sparingly for the best effect.

TOUCH-UPS ■

As we all know from frustrating experience, paint left in cans doesn't keep well. There's a better way. Store leftover paint in mason jars with two-part screw-on tops, labeled with the paint name and color. Every six months or so, shake the jar and turn it upside down.

(**ReWard:** Do it when you rotate your art, accessories, and throw-pillows.)

When you need to do a quick touch-up, apply the paint with a damp (not wet) cotton swab. This works beautifully with both flat and semi-gloss paints, but if you attempt to touch up eggshell on an eggshell wall, you'll end up with a visible semi-gloss spot.

Wallpaper

Although wallpaper is more expensive than paint, it can easily conceal imperfect walls and provide a colorful, textural backdrop for your room.

Traditionalists have favored wallpaper for centuries and still do. Toile, damask, and moiré are good choices for homes that are filled with period furnishings. More contemporary spaces can use simpler, clean-lined papers that have a textured stone or marbleized look. In kitchens and bathrooms, vinyl wallpaper is strong and can be wiped down without damage.

If you already have a vinyl wallpaper hung in your home and are thinking about painting over it, check to see that the seams are secure. If they are, apply one coat of oil-based primer/sealer. Twenty-four hours later, you can paint over it using one or two coats of oil-based or latex paint.

If you don't own your home but want a wallpaper accent, use one of the many wallpaper borders that are available. Generally it's best not to use a border in the living room. They're most effective in less formal rooms, such as the kitchen, bedroom, or hallway.

Floors, Rugs, and Carpets

Wood Floors

If you have exposed wood floors, you need to keep them in good condition—even if you rent. Scrape and stain them (or leave them natural), but protect them with two or three coats of water-based polyurethane. Every other year after that, add another two coats of polyurethane for additional protection.

Remember not to use water on your wood floors. A good wood floor cleaner will make them look even better and last longer.

Another option is to pickle a wood floor, which can make a room look lighter and larger. Just use the minimum amount of white pickling stain needed so that the natural grain of the wood shows through.

And, of course, wood floors can be painted with an overall pattern, with a decorative border, or from wall to wall, in a uniform color. Look for special polyurethane, oil-based paint for porches and floors. Painted floors are a particularly good alternative in a dining area in lieu of a carpet (which is generally something of a crumb catcher as well as an obstacle when it comes to moving chairs in and out).

Rugs and Carpets

If you have good wood floors in your social rooms, use rugs to define space, such as a conversation area. You have options, depending on the size of your room. A 6' x 9' rug can be used inside the conversation space, an 8' x 10' rug can tuck under the front legs of your chairs and sofa, and a 9' x 12' rug can be placed under the entire seating arrangement.

In a bedroom with a wood floor, you can use a pair of runners on either side of the bed. They should measure 2½' to 3' wide by 4' long.

Rugs made in any number of materials, from nylon to silk, come in a wide range of prices, from inexpensive to heirloom. Persian rugs offer lots of burgundy and navy hues, as well as neutrals blended with browns. Swedish rugs tend to come in more geometric patterns and meld well with contemporary furnishings. Chinese rugs, especially Art Deco Chinese, contain a lot of green and plum. Tibetan rugs are also popular because of their neutral palette and their sleek sophisticated patterns, as are needlepoint Aubusson rugs.

As far as carpeting is concerned, you also have a lot of choices. Today, many manufacturers have adapted commercial carpeting for the home. Flatter and easier to maintain than traditional residential carpeting, it wears well. If you have children or your home has heavy traffic, commercial carpeting is the most practical choice. You can have nylon carpeting cut to the size you need. It can be self-edged, or a 2" grosgrain ribbon or leather border can be added to extend its boundaries. Tie it into one of the colors in your fabric.

If your budget allows for it, wool carpet is certainly a terrific option too, as it is strong and cleans beautifully.

Good carpeting can be "recycled" when you move. You can have the section of your bedroom carpet that's been under the bed cut out and bound to use as an area rug in your new home.

Tiles

If you own your home, ceramic tile flooring is an excellent alternative to wood or carpeting for high-traffic areas. Glazed tiles are easier on the feet than very porous terra-cotta tiles, which do not allow the foot to glide. Use 1" to 12" tiles in bathrooms and 4" to 12" tiles in the kitchen. A good rule: the larger the space, the bigger the tile. Entrance foyers become instantly elegant with an installation of marble tile—a little goes a long way. Travertine, a creamy neutral, is the least expensive marble available and works well in any style home.

Vinyl tile works well in kitchens, as does vinyl sheet linoleum. Both are easy to clean and affordable. Given the choice, I prefer vinyl tiles for most applications—especially the classic black and white checkerboard, stonelike tiles, or marbleized 12" squares, which always look sophisticated.

Window Treatments

Few elements of interior design seem to confuse people as much as window treatments because windows vary so much from house to house. The question of decor, the amount of privacy required, how much light to allow in or block out, and whether or not there is a view are all questions that need to be addressed.

Wooden venetian blinds, in wide (my preference) or narrow slats, are a terrific choice. They look chic in a study, library, or bedroom.

You can find wooden blinds in lots of finishes, from lightly pickled to dark mahogany. Their fabric tapes, which come in a wide range of colors, can be coordinated with the fabric on upholstered furniture. In a kitchen, for example, white blinds with red tape can immediately brighten and bring cheer. Make sure the cord is on the less conspicuous side (and, in the kitchen, away from the stove).

Metal blinds, which are still ubiquitous in office settings, have a harder look to them. Lately, with so many homeowners leaving the high-tech look behind in favor of a warmer, cozier feel, they are not used as much for residential interiors.

Shutters can darken a room well and offer a lot of privacy. Standard-size shutters are best for smaller rooms and are compatible with country-style interiors. Painted white or stained dark, these window treatments work well in libraries, too. For larger eclectic or contemporary-style rooms, wide plantation shutters, from floor to ceiling, can make quite a dramatic statement. Shutters can be costly because they are generally custom-made but make truly elegant window coverings.

Sheer curtains can be used in many situations. Not only do they allow light in, they offer privacy as well. Sheers can flow to a windowsill or the floor. When gathered together on rods inside the top and bottom of a window frame, they can offer additional privacy. Choose a plain sheer, without any pattern, that doesn't draw attention to itself and away from the room. It will give you a soft, dreamy impression of the view outside.

Lined curtains in heavier fabrics will always remain a beloved classic, but more and more people are opting for a lighter look, requiring less maintenance, even in the winter months. If you choose to use a lined fabric on your windows, hang it on wooden or metal poles with coordinated rings and finials for a more polished look. This option is usually not sufficient without additional window treatment. Lined curtains that are swagged or simply hang straight down to the floor require another covering over the actual window such as shades or blinds. Most of the treatments mentioned here will do, with the exception of balloon or Roman shades.

Balloon shades work best in traditional homes. These romantic shades block more light and view in the "up" position than any other treatments because they cover one-third to one half of a window's top surface at all times. Bedrooms are the best place for these fabric-heavy treatments.

Roman shades give more light control while using less fabric. They can be made from a dreamy, gauzy material that allows a lot of light in or heavy cotton duck or canvas that will block light.

Bamboo blinds in a tortoiseshell finish have become a classic. Hung with lined curtains in a traditional home, they add an air of elegance. Hung alone, they convey a tropical look. In country houses or second homes, *matchstick blinds* are an inexpensive alternative that are easy to maintain. It's best to hang these blinds inside the window frame, even if there are no curtains, for a custom-size fit.

Duette® shades are very popular, for good reason. Available in transparent, semi-opaque, opaque, and blackout densities, these custom-made pleated honeycomb shades have built-in dust and soil repellents. Light sleepers especially appreciate their blackout shades, which block out 99.5 percent of light. This is also a good option for windows that don't have a deep frame or windowsill. Duette shades can even be used on greenhouse and fanlight windows.

Their dual control, which allows owners to have the top "down" or the bottom part "up," is an added plus. For instance, if you live on a street close to another house or building, or one that has a lot of passing traffic, keeping the bottom half of the window covered while the top is down will offer you privacy while still allowing light and sky in. Duette shades come in small, medium, and large pleats and a number of colors. For the best effect, choose one that matches your wall color.

Silhouette® shades are one of my favorites. These ideal shades, also custom-made, are soil and dust repellent like the Duette shades, and can transform a room very quickly by offering a lot of flexibility. If you have a view, the transparent mode adds a note of softness, giving the effect of a sheer curtain. If privacy is an issue, they will give you maximum coverage: by simply pulling a cord they will become opaque. Bon Soir Silhouette shades are available for the bedroom. Constructed with denser center blinds, they offer greater opacity.

Silhouette shades require just 3¼" of depth to be hung inside a window frame; otherwise, they can be hung outside of it. Available in lots of colors, they are most effective when matched to your wall color, giving a smooth, soft transition between your windows and walls (see Sources).

Luminette® vertical blinds are most appropriate on a sliding door or with a sliding door and window combination. The effect is just like that of a Silhouette shade.

A Before-and-After Story:

The Top-to-Bottom
Transformation

Olivia and Bill's Philadelphia apartment, which had
been hers prior to their marriage, is a really good example of how changing the configuration of the furniture alone was not sufficient. To make this room work

optimally, we had to make some subtle but important—although not terribly expensive—changes to the shell.

The living room in this modern high-rise apartment doubled as a workspace; the desk and computer were housed in a tall armoire that sat side by side with a small chest. Opposite, the club chair with matching ottoman and the sofa were arranged too far from each other to make conversation comfortable. The single brass table lamp, which was on an end table that is hidden in this photo, did not provide sufficient lighting for the entire room. A white lace valance, hanging above the window, did nothing to enhance either the window or the room. The country-style windowpane mirror to the left of the sofa was too small and feminine for the room. The only other piece of art was a framed print hung on a short wall next to the window.

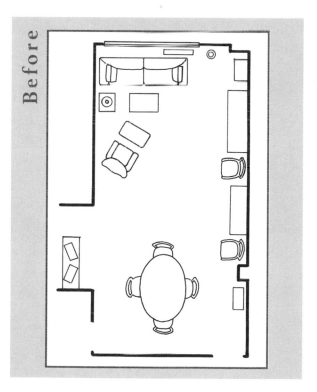

Before

Other Common Mistakes

- **Uncomfortable conversation area**

Clue: **Look at the distance between the chair and the sofa.**

- **Furniture of different heights**

Clue: **Look at the height of the armoire.**

- **Room that lacks a cohesive look**

Clue: **Can you find any pairs?**

- **Ignoring a room's focal point**

Clue: **Can you find one?**

- **Improper use of artwork**

Clue: **Look at the print hidden in the corner.**

- **Ineffective use of accessories**

Clue: **Look at the coffee table.**

- **Using lighting incorrectly**

Clue: **Is one lamp sufficient?**

What We Banished

- **Wicker trunk (coffee table)**
- **Windowpane mirror**
- **Small framed print**
- **Dining room bookcase**
- **Large audio speakers**
- **Hanging brass lighting fixture (in dining room)**
- **Wall-to-wall carpeting**
- **Lace valance**

What We Borrowed

- **Japanese painting**

The dining area of this room had a chaotic look because of the messy bookcase topped with large speakers. Also, the fixture above the table was too small and didn't provide adequate light. The artwork was hung where it could not be fully appreciated.

■

These problems were easily remedied with a quick re-arrangement of the furniture. But what really needed attention, first, was the shell. The whole place needed to be painted. In addition, the carpeting was faded and there was some minor structural work that was required to make the room more functional and graceful.

The most dramatic changes in the living room were accomplished simply by moving the furniture. We created an intimate conversation area with the sage green slipcovered sofa placed on the long wall, flanked by the end table on one side and a new tree on the other. The height of the tree balanced the vertical line of the armoire situated diagonally across the

room. The club chair and ottoman were separated to provide additional seating and a new coffee table was placed in between them. Two new brass floor lamps provided much needed lighting.

On the right wall of the living room, the armoire and the small cabinet, which had been tucked in the corner, were switched for the console and two chairs from the dining area, which could be used for additional seating.

The framed limited edition poster from the foyer was now displayed on the console along with the brass lamp to

What We Bought

- Built-in window storage
- Wall-to-wall carpeting
- Window treatment
- Two brass floor lamps
- A coffee table
- Sofa slipcover
- A tree
- Decorative wall brackets
- Throw and floor pillows
- Tabletop accessories
- Built-in storage closet
- Track lighting
- Brass hardware

After

complete the focal point. A Japanese painting that had been in the bedroom was hung over the sofa. Two gold-leaf brackets flanked it, creating more drama. The round taupe cushion on the floor added a whimsical note.

In addition, the room had been transformed by an ivory Silhouette® shade at the window that matched the creamy paint color on the walls. We decided to use the chair's softer palette of taupe, cream, and sage throughout the room. A taupe nylon sisal wall-to-wall carpet was installed.

An under-the-window air conditioner and radiator, which were once hidden behind the sofa, were now exposed after the furniture was rearranged and an awkward recessed jog to the right of the window emphasized how off-center the window actually was. The answer—a built-in unit that housed everything and provided lots of welcome closed storage. Formerly an eyesore, the transformed window area added to the newly serene environment.

The biggest change in the dining area was a new built-in, floor-to-ceiling cabinet, to replace the bookcase. Not only did it add more storage space, it also gave the area a sleeker, more sophisticated look. In addition, it increased the resale value of their home.

Track lighting supplied much-needed illumination and was less obtrusive than the small hanging lamp. It also provided the new workspace (in the armoire on the left) with extra light. Note that because there are so many doors in this area (and lack of wall space), no art was used here. Again, the fresh paint and carpeting spruced up the entire area. And finally, new brass doorknobs and pulls were added for a bit of shine.

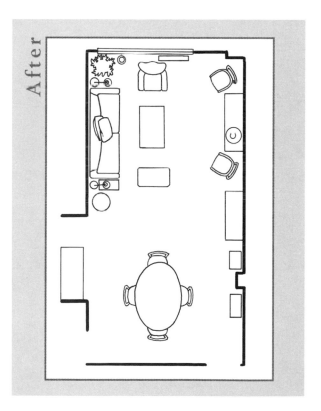

ABOUT RADIATOR COVERS ■

If you live in an older home or apartment and have a radiator (or air conditioner) in front of your window, seriously consider covering it up. Don't, however, purchase one of those stock radiator covers with the metal grill in the front, unless you're renting for a short period of time. (All they do is draw even more attention. If you already have a stock cover be sure to paint it the same color as the surrounding walls, using special radiator paint on the metal grill if it's in the front.)

You can create extra storage space and hide the radiator at the same time by building a unit, from wall to wall, under the window and up to or

over the windowsill, which will contain closed storage and cover the radiator simultaneously. These built-ins should have doors with touch latches—no hardware—to keep the unit unobtrusive. To finish it, prime and paint the built-in with the same semi-gloss paint as the trim in the room. This window built-in can also be a great window seat, too.

Your Shell Checklist

To give your shell the care it deserves, consider the following:

- Have you checked the paint, wall coverings, window treatments, and flooring in your room(s)?

- Have you determined what kind of paint—flat, eggshell, semi-gloss, or high-gloss—will work best?

- Is wallpaper an alternative for you?

- If you have wood floors, are they in good condition?

- Have you determined whether you'd like to use area rugs or carpeting?

- Are you clear about which window treatment will work best for you?

- If your radiator or air conditioner is visible, have you thought about enclosing it?

- Are you comfortable?

Chapter Twelve

Live Well
in Every Room

Throughout this book, I've used living rooms to illustrate design principles, for the most part. But, of course, every room in your home is important and should be as inviting and comfortable as possible. Although the foyer, kitchen, family room, bedroom, and bathroom all serve specific functions, there are lots of things you can do to improve them. No matter how big or small your space is, you can effect dramatic changes by altering just a few things in each room.

The Foyer

Whether it's a few square feet, a small vestibule, or a grand and formal entrance, the foyer gives the first impression of what your home looks like.

The most useful piece of furniture to have in a foyer is a small chest (or console) that provides closed storage, with either two or three shelves or drawers. It's a great place to keep those outerwear accessories like gloves, scarves, and hats. (Any furniture or shelves in the foyer should have rounded corners since this is a highly trafficked area.)

If space allows, have one or two chairs flanking the chest or console. It's a convenient location for pulling boots on and off as well as a place for an older person to sit down. (These chairs are also handy as extra seating to move

into the dining or living room as needed.) You might consider slipcovers for these side chairs. (ReWard: Slipcovers can be changed seasonally to give you a fresh look.)

Alternatively, if you have room only for a shelf, keep in mind that it doesn't have to be very large. One that is only five inches deep will provide space for a small tray and vase of flowers. Hang a mirror above it and you'll create a more welcoming area for you and your guests.

The Millers' house in Salt Lake City had an entrance foyer with wonderful architectural details—the stone wall and trio of windows—but they were overshadowed by the eclectic mix of furniture and accessories, none of which really worked together.

A Before-and-After Story:

Making a Grand Entrance

A small hinged box to hold keys or change makes an attractive and useful accessory in the foyer. (I like a hinged box because the top flips back and doesn't have to be removed, thereby taking up additional space.) If there isn't room for a box, use a small silver or brass tray instead. I advise against displaying accessories of porcelain or glass here since there is a greater risk that they may get broken in a high-traffic area.

If your foyer has the room, tuck a metal umbrella stand (in a finish that complements the other materials in the space) into a corner. To add more interest, you can add a few antique and new walking sticks with amusing handles.

Just as we're using garden ornaments as interior accessories, outdoor furniture, such as a wooden or cast iron garden bench, can be a practical alternative indoors, too.

And don't forget your front door. Doorknobs can be changed to coordinate with the metal that is being used in the foyer. Old-fashioned security chains can be replaced with the brass or chrome latches used on hotel guest room doors. I love the brass or chrome covers that fit right over the lock and give the door a cleaner, more elegant appearance. (See Sources for more on hardware.)

After

In the study, we found a simple black table with a maple top. Its clean lines blended well with the foyer space. Simply by adding a few Asian-inspired accent pieces, the architecture was enhanced and the space felt more serene.

The Kitchen

One complaint I hear from every client with whom I've worked is that their kitchens don't have enough counter and floor space. Clearly, it's at a premium, especially in many apartments. However, there are easy and effective ways to create more space and, in the process, make everything look a lot better.

Three Simple Steps to End Kitchen Clutter

- Remove every small appliance on the counter that you don't use on a daily basis, and store it. (You'll free up lots of counter space immediately, which is especially important if you have a small kitchen.)
- Invest in a concealed garbage pail that hangs inside a cabinet door or rolls out on a track. By "hiding" the garbage and getting it off the floor, the kitchen will immediately look better and feel bigger.
- If you have a dishwasher, get rid of the dish drainer and board on the countertop; it takes up lots of space. If you really need a drainer, invest in the collapsible kind that can be stored away easily.

Small Things That Make a Big Difference

- To streamline your kitchen even more, consider installing a three-way gooseneck faucet on the sink (so that large pasta and soup pots can fit under it easily), with a sprayer and a liquid soap dispenser.
- For a quick, bright punch of color in an all-white kitchen, choose one accent color or metal finish and change all of your hardware to it.
- If you have an eat-in kitchen, consider using a round pedestal table and armless chairs, which will allow you more flexibility and

Filled with herbs, this clean-lined white flower box enhances the window and provides a touch of green year round.

freedom of movement. (In small kitchens, round tables offer more comfortable seating than square or rectangular tables.)

- In the kitchen (and bathroom), all paper products should be white, without a pattern. Not only is this ecologically sound, it will give the room a less chaotic look.

Minor Renovations

- If you have a stainless steel sink that doesn't have a soap dispenser (check to see if yours has a precut hole that is capped), you can have one installed and do away with the soap bottle cluttering the counter.
- Remember—I can't say it enough—make sure that all counter corners, as well as those of the table, are rounded. You'll avoid bruises and feel more comfortable.

- **Uncomfortable conversation area**

Clue: **Do the seats look comfortable?**

- **Improper use of art**

Clue: **Do the aprons count as art?**

- **Ineffective use of accessories**

Clue: **Look at the countertop.**

A Before-and-After Story:

Creating a Cozier Kitchen

Chris and Pat's Kansas City kitchen was big, open, and airy, but there were several design mistakes that contributed to a cluttered look and uncomfortable feel of the room: a cluster of fridge magnets, aprons hanging on the wall, poor choice of lighting fixture, and a too-small recycling pail all detracted from this kitchen's positive features.

Also, Chris complained that the stools and chairs were very uncomfortable and that she was tired of the mica table.

Although the kitchen looks dramatically different, keep in mind that the changes were cosmetic, and no significant renovations were made.

The countertops were cleared of seldom-used appliances. The small chrome pail that was being used for recy-

What We Banished

- "Butcher block" countertops
- Chrome chairs and stools
- Mica table
- Small pail
- Aprons
- Light fixture
- Fridge magnets
- Seldom-used small appliances

What We Borrowed

- An ivy plant
- A painting

What We Bought

- Corian countertops
- Antique table
- Wooden chairs and cushions
- Wooden stools

clables was replaced by a larger covered copper tub that the couple already had. We "de-cluttered" by removing the fridge magnets and the aprons dangling on the wall. The owners decided to change the table to an antique wooden one that matched the cabinets' wood trim. They also purchased four new chairs and two simple wooden stools that were more comfortable and compatible than the old ones. The suspended light fixture, which was too modern to be paired with the antique table and wooden chairs, was replaced with additional recessed lighting installed directly over the table. The only "renovation" made was to change the Formica butcher block counter to white Corian so that it no longer clashed with the wood trim of the cabinets. A large hanging ivy plant was displayed above a seldom-used cabinet for a touch of green.

The "Family" Room

Many of the homes I visit have both living rooms and family rooms. Oftentimes the use of the rooms overlap, and owners end up with two areas that have almost identical functions and looks. If this applies to you, I suggest that you go back to the very first principle in this book: defining priorities. As you review the questionnaire that appears at the end of chapter 1, you will quickly uncover the specific functions of these two rooms, which will then lead you to making the correct decisions about how to change them and how to make the distinction between them.

As you look at each room separately, you will want to follow all of the guidelines throughout this book, but your choices of what to place in each room, such as furnishings, art, accessories, etc., will be determined by the look and feel you want for each space.

Some points come quickly to mind: the study or family room should be the more informal of the two, for watching television and other family activities. This is the room for a more casual fabric or leather sofa, for the entertainment center, for family photos on the walls. Then the living room can be the more elegant room—no matter what its style—suitable for conversation, entertaining, and reading. In the living room, you'll want to use finer fabrics on the furnishings, formal wall and window finishes, fine art, silver, and crystal. (But I still admonish everyone not to make the living room into a museum because not only will you want to entertain here, you'll want to use this room as a blissful personal refuge in which you feel completely at ease for quiet times.)

THE SOFA BED ■

If you have a sofa bed that you don't use on a regular basis, be sure to place it so that the *seating* arrangement is comfortable. Don't worry if the bed, when it's opened, doesn't leave much room for traffic—it's only temporary. It should not deter you from having the most functional and attractive room possible on a day-to-day basis.

The Bedroom

The bedroom is the place where you probably spend more time than in any other room of the house, although you might be asleep for most of those hours. But this room presents many challenges because what you do with this space is dictated, for the most part, by its function. The common decorating mistakes made by most people in their bedroom are: lack of cohesion, improper use of artwork, ineffective use of accessories, and using lighting incorrectly.

Most obviously, this is the room for sleeping, and the average bed—double, queen, or king size—will dominate the room, and it generally is the focal point. The placement of the bed is the first decision to be made. And, following the guidelines we used in arranging the living room, the longest wall in the bedroom is the place to start. If the longest wall is *across* from the door, you will have the ideal set up to allow the best traffic flow to and around the bed (which makes for easier bed making, also).

As you know so well by now, balance is crucial to achieve a cohesive look, so use pairs. Flank the bed with end tables and a pair of lamps, matching or as much alike as possible. You can use two different tables if they are of the same height and wood tone, or two different lamps of similar sizes, dressed with matching shades, to affect a pair.

More often than not, people use too much art in the bedroom to be effective. Bedrooms simply need one or perhaps two large pieces over the bed (as a focal point) to avoid visual chaos—the last thing you want in this room.

Bedroom accessories should be pared down, too. Start with your bedside tables, which should as free of clutter as possible. A reading lamp, a clock radio, a telephone, and perhaps a framed photo or a vase of fresh flowers are all that should be left out. The reason is not only practical but aesthetic: with less "mess" there's more space and a more peaceful environment.

Bedside tables with closed storage or drawers will give you space for a small box of tissues, a cup of tea, an address/phone book, a pen or pencil, glasses, and whatever else you need to have at hand. You can use the top of a bureau for a collection of objects or photographs.

Don't forget those swing-arm lamps. A pair will free up the table surfaces, and provide excellent reading light. (And speaking of light, consider using battery-operated lights that can be mounted to illuminate dark clothing closets without going to the expense of rewiring.)

Although I recommend the bedroom be a work-free space, it is sometimes the only available spot for your home office. You can hide the work space inside an armoire or a wall unit or behind a decorative screen. By keeping paperwork and your computer out of sight, you'll be able to keep your mind on more pleasurable bedroom activities.

A Before-and-After Story:

Bedroom Redux

S ean's decidedly "undecorated" bedroom had a lot of light and handy storage under the window, but the room needed some refinement now that it was being shared with his new wife, Sarah. Between them, they already had all the furniture they needed; it was simply a matter of changing art and accessories and enhancing the bedding, lighting, and window treatments.

A few inexpensive changes transformed the room. To begin with, a small oil painting that had been hung too high next to the window was removed. Although I recommend leaving window walls free of art, the couple had no other wall space available, so we hung one of their favorite lithographs lower down on the wall. (Their happiness was my priority.) The headboard, formerly upholstered in seafoam green ottoman fabric, was slipcovered in a cream silk with black welting, and a dustskirt was made to match. New pillows—two large European squares with black tailored shams, a long bolster with the same cream silk fabric and black welt, and two accent pillows—joined the two standard (sleeping) pillows. A satin striped duvet cover was used to conceal the down comforter. New wooden tops were added to the bedside tables for a more polished look. A second, matching lamp was purchased to create a pair for the bedside tables. And we limited accessories to a clock, the phone, and a few decorative items. Finally, sheer curtains were hung to soften the city view.

HOW TO MAKE A BED ■

You already know that a bed will always be the focal point of any bedroom. Therefore, its prominence dictates that the colors and styles of the bedding you choose should be integrated with the overall design of the room whether it's traditional, modern, or eclectic. The choices you make are limited only by your imagination. But with so many choices available, there are still some common guidelines—tricks of the trade—that designers use to achieve the look you see in magazines and store showrooms.

Here follow basic components to create your (pardon the expression) "decorator-look" bed:

- A dust skirt

- Fitted and flat sheets

- A comforter (instead of a flat blanket) with a duvet cover (ReWard: This cover can be changed seasonally, as you do your slipcovers, towels, and art)

- Two "European" 26" square pillows with shams (one for a twin bed)

- Two standard or king-size pillows

- Two neckrolls or one breakfast pillow

Make your bed as you normally would—dust skirt, fitted sheet, flat sheet, and the covered comforter. Then, fold the flat sheet and the comforter back at least seven inches from the top of the bed. Stand the two European square pillows up against the headboard or wall. (They can have the points up if you wish.) Then place the standard or king-size pillows upright in front of them, followed by the small pillows. These small pillows can be in an accent color or match the others.

If you have an upholstered chair in the bedroom, you can have the neckroll or breakfast pillow done in the same fabric for a custom look.

The Bathroom

I believe that the bathroom should feel spalike—pristine, clean, and light. Dark colors and busy patterns for wallpapers, shower curtains, and accessories should be avoided since they inevitably make a room look smaller. Reserve the patterns and vivid colors for towels since they can be used to change the look of a bathroom seasonally or as the mood strikes you: darker, richer hues work for the winter and the paler, softer tones for the summer. Fluffy white towels with a contrasting monogram are classics that work year-round.

I always suggest that if you own your home it's a good idea to get rid of shower curtains and liners—they get mildewy and obscure at least a third of the room—and replace them with a clear glass tub-and-shower enclosure that is installed on the existing tub. With it, you can see the room from wall to wall or window. They are easy to clean, don't have to be replaced, enlarge the space, and enhance the resale value of your home. If you're a renter, use a solid textured shower curtain in terry cloth, cotton duck, or moiré for a stylish look.

Unless you already own a beautiful pedestal sink, I recommend that you install a closed vanity under the sink. It will provide extra storage space while hiding all of your toiletries from view. There are lots of styles to choose from—a stained wooden vanity with a drop-in porcelain sink for traditional-style homes to an all stainless steel vanity and drop-in sink for more modern homes.

Choose one metal finish for the bathroom and use it consistently throughout the room (i.e., the faucets, flusher, and toilet paper holder). That includes accessories, too. The soap dish on the sink, the tissue box cover (get the boutique-size tissues—they take up less space), drinking cups, and waste pails can be found, for instance, in stainless steel and brass. Again, metal is durable and easy to maintain. (No plastic, please.)

"Cutesy" things in bathrooms only add clutter. Remove crocheted tissue box holders, tiny guest soaps, and anything that is not related to a function of the room. Just keep a soap dish on the sink and a caddy in the shower to hold shampoo, conditioner, loofahs, and anything else you use.

The bathroom deserves good art, too. Hang one piece of fine art that you will feel comfortable with there, either over the towel bar or above the toilet. Make sure that it's framed, and is no smaller than 8" × 10". (Even though this is a small room, you don't want to add to the clutter with tiny pieces of art on the walls.)

Let's all do our best to eliminate the following ubiquitous detractors.

- **Lucite frames.** Please use any type but these.

- **Fridge magnets.** Using these are the fastest way to give your kitchen a messy look. Unless you have a serious collection, please put them all away.

- **Cluttered windowsills.** With the exception of indoor flower boxes, always leave windowsills clear; your room will look a lot tidier.

- **Doilies.** Whether they are crocheted or linen, please remove these dust collectors.

- **Patterned and colored toilet paper, napkins, and paper towels.** Buy plain white. Don't let the paper manufacturers dictate your style.

- **Big audio speakers.** If they're on the floor, they're too big. (No matter what the man in your life says, you don't really need them.) Purchase small white speakers (Bose or Aiwa) to put in the wall unit or hang in corners near the ceiling.

- **Cutesy bathroom bric-a-brac.** Use only those things that add to a spalike environment.

- **The same rug, wallpaper, or fabric in more than one room of the house.** Let each room be an original.

- **Liquid detergent bottles on kitchen countertops.** If you don't have a built-in sink dispenser, get a stainless steel pump container for a sleeker look.

- **"Do not remove" tags on throw pillows.** It's safe to remove them now.

 # Your Final
ReWard

Now that you know how to use what you have most effectively, you can transform your home—and any home you have in the future—so it will reach its full potential. In this way, you too will be making the world a more beautiful place.

When I was a little girl my mother would recite:

> *Good, better, best*
> *Never let it rest.*
> *Until the good is better*
> *And the better is the best!*

I'd Love to See
Your Before-and-Afters

Before-and-after photographs are a wonderful way to record the dramatic changes that can be made to any home—that's why I've included so many of them in this book. Before you move a single piece of furniture, take out the camera. You'll be glad you did. And, if you'd like to share them with me, please send prints or slides to:

USE-WHAT-YOU-HAVE INTERIORS®
109 EAST 73RD STREET
NEW YORK, NY 10021-3571

For more information about our Seminars, Consultations, and The Interior Refiners Network® (Decorator Training Program), please visit our Website: www.redecorate.com or call 800-WE-USE-IT.®

Sources

Lighting

PAR-3 Halogen Track Lighting

  Lightolier, Inc.
  800-544-5983

Cord-Control Kit

  Hold Everything
  Catalog
  800-421-2264

Lamp Shades and Lighting

  Shades of Light
  Catalog
  800-262-6612

Tree Uplights

  Frontgate Catalog
  800-626-6488

Dimmers

  Lutron Electronics
  800-523-9466

Clamp Lamps

  Sam Flax, NYC
  212-620-3010

Reading Lamps

  Levenger Catalog
  800-544-0880

Assorted Lighting

  The Lighting Center,
  NYC
  212-888-8388

  Lee's Studio, NYC
  212-581-4400

Paint

Benjamin Moore Paints

  Stores Nationwide
  888-236-6667

Ralph Lauren Paint Collection

  Stores Nationwide
  800-379-7656

Stamping Kit

  Ballard Design
  800-367-2775

Window Treatments

Silhouette® Duette® and Luminette® Shades

  Hunter Douglas
  800-943-STYLE

Window Hardware

  Smith & Noble
  Catalog
  800-248-8888

Window Treatments

  Rue de France
  Catalog
  800-777-0998

Furniture

Assorted Furnishings

Crate & Barrel
Catalog
800-451-8217

Exposures Homes
Catalog
800-699-6993

Pottery Barn
800-922-5507

*Indoor/Outdoor
Furniture*

Gardners Eden
Catalog
800-822-9600

Decorative Screens

Gump's Catalog
800-284-8677

Wicker Furnishings

Pier 1 Imports
800-447-4371

Fabric

Fabrics

IDC Signature
Textiles
888-4-TEXTILES

*Fabrics and Home
Accessories*

ABC Carpet &
Home, NYC
212-473-3000

Fringe and Tassels

M & J Trimmings,
NYC
212-391-9072

Kitchen and Bath

Bistro Tables and Chairs

Smith & Hawken
Catalog
415-389-8300

*Rack-Sack® Concealed
Pail*

Bed, Bath & Beyond
800-GO-BEYOND

Bathroom Accessories

Chambers Catalog
800-334-9790

*Kitchen and Bathroom
Accessories*

Solutions Catalog
800-342-9988

Williams-Sonoma
Catalog
800-541-2233

Bedroom

Comforters and Linens

The Company Store
Catalog
800-285-3696

Vanity Stools, Linens

Horchow Fine Linen
Catalog
800-456-7000

Art

*Frames, Mats, Wall
Brackets*

Exposures Catalog
800-222-4947

Hardware

*Brass or Chrome Lock
Covers, etc.*

Gracious Home, NYC
800-338-7809

Simons, NYC
212-532-9220

A

Accent lighting, 169–70, 177
Accent pillows, 53
Accessories, 6, 21, 25, 27, 59, 93,
    106–11, 135–59
    candles, 156–58, 159
    CD holders and wine racks,
    158
    checklist for, 159
    clocks, 158
    dealing with, 137–39, 159
    in dining room, 144–48
    displaying of, 142–43
    fruit bowls, 158
    pairs of, 91
    plants, 153–55, 159
    three secrets of, 137
    throw pillows, 155, 159
Area rugs, 39, 41, 47
Armoires, 67, 79, 114, 115,
    149
Art-free zones, 118
Artwork, 6, 25, 27, 35, 75, 83,
    93, 97, 98, 109, 145, 217.
    See also Photographs
    balance and, 120, 134
    breathing space for, 119
    checklist for, 134
    as focal point, 113, 114, 115
    frames and, 125–26, 134
    groups of, 117, 121–23, 134
    hanging, 126
    on more than one wall, 122
    pairs of, 89
    placing, 31, 33, 47, 49, 51, 52,
    53, 55, 57, 78, 116–34
    seasons and, 118, 134
    in various rooms, 130–33
    wallpaper and, 133

B

Audio equipment, 15, 218
    wall units for, 35, 39, 49

Balance, 6, 35, 37, 63–79, 83,
    103, 120, 143
    chairs and, 65–66, 69, 70,
    76–77
    checklist for, 79
    definition and importance of,
    63–64
    large pieces and, 67, 79
    slipcovers and, 65
    sofas and loveseats and, 64–65,
    69, 70, 76–77
"Banished, borrowed, and
    bought" lists, 7–8
Bathrooms, 216–17, 218
    art in, 132, 217
    lighting in, 177
Bed-making tips, 214–15
Bedrooms, 210–15
    art in, 132
    focal points in, 114
    lighting in, 175–76
Bedside tables, 91
Before-and-after photos, 7,
    220
Blinds and shades, 189–91
Bookcases/bookshelves, 25, 59,
    60, 115, 150–52
    accessories and artwork on,
    27
    arranging by book height rec-
    ommended for, 151, 152, 159
    balance and, 67
    placing of, 38–39, 47, 48–49
Butler's tables, 37–38

C

Candelabra, 57, 107
Candles, 156–58, 159
Carpets, 188–89. *See also* Rugs
CD holders, 158
CFLs (compact fluorescent light-
    bulbs), 176
"Chair-and-a-half," 65
Chairs:
    balance and, 65–66, 69, 70,
    76–77
    club, 65
    in pairs, 89, 91
    placing of, 22–23, 29, 30–31,
    33, 38, 41, 45, 47, 48, 55, 62
    slipper, 65
    upholstered, 18, 19, 34, 65
    wooden, 65
Chandeliers, 164–66, 177
Chanel, Coco, 118
Chests, 67, 93, 114
Children, 14, 48
Churchill, Sir Winston, *xiii*
Clocks, 57, 106, 158
Club chairs, 65
Coffee tables, 18, 19, 40, 60
    accessories placed on, 141
    placing of, 22–23, 29, 31, 34,
    41, 47, 48, 51, 52, 55
    sharp edges on, 45
Cohesive look, 6, 88–96
    checklist for, 96
    creation of, 92–95
    pairs and, 88, 89–91
Comfort, 15, 16, 41, 53, 66, 79,
    115, 159
Compact fluorescent lightbulbs
    (CFLs), 176
Computers, 15

Console tables, 56
Conversation areas, 6, 16–41, 43,
  69, 70, 75, 76, 77, 83, 97,
  109, 115, 117, 145
  checklist for, 41
  creating flow in, 24–27
  finding center of, 28–31
  form and function in, 32–
  35
  four goals of, 18
  must-haves for, 19
  "screaming distance" in, 16–17,
  20–23, 29
Cooney, Barbara, 9
Cove lighting, 164

D

Decorating mistakes, ten most
  common, 6
Dimmers, 173
Dining rooms:
  accessories in, 144–48
  art in, 130–31
  focal points in, 112–13, 115
  living rooms combined with,
  56, 58–61, 115
Dining tables, 43, 58–61
Doilies, 218
"Do not remove" tags, 218
Don't use what you have top
  ten, 218
Doorways, 45
Dracaena trees, 30
Drop-leaf tables, 56

E

End tables, 34, 37, 39, 45, 47,
  48, 51, 62, 79, 93–94, 114,
  141
  importance and selection of,
  67
  pairs of, 91
Entertaining, 14, 15, 17
"Eye level," 116

F

Family patterns, repetition of,
  16–17
Family rooms, 208–9
Fireplaces, 18, 30–31, 55, 76, 97,
  98
Floors, wood, 187–88

Focal points, 6, 21, 47, 69, 83,
  97–115, 145
  in bedrooms, 114
  checklist for, 115
  collections as, 106–11
  in dining rooms, 112–13, 115
  establishing, 18, 30–31, 35, 52,
  53, 76, 97–115
  finding natural, 98–99
  in foyers, 114
Form and function, 32–35
Foyers, 200–203
Frames, 125–26, 148
Fruit bowls, 158
Furniture placement, 6, 42–62
  checklist for, 62
  of modular units, 50–53
  traffic flow patterns and, 18,
  24–27, 43–45
  "wallflower rooms" and, 42–43,
  46–49

G

Glass tables, 40
Grand pianos, 18, 51, 107

H

Halogen spot lights, 162–63, 177
Hardware on accessories, 157,
  159
Hoffmann, Josef, 58
Hoffmann furniture, 58–59
Home beautification, 179–218
  room by room, 200–218
  of the shell, 181–99
Home offices, 15, 211

K

Kitchens, 204–7
  creating coziness in, 206–7
  ending clutter in, 204
  lighting in, 176
  minor renovations in, 205
Kitchen tables, 43

L

Lampshades, 165, 170, 172
Lighting, 6, 47, 93, 109, 160–77
  accent, 169–70, 177
  in bathrooms, 177

in bedrooms, 175–76
chandeliers, 164–66, 177
checklist for, 177
with compact fluorescent
  lightbulbs, 176
cord control kits for, 171
cove, 164
dimmers, outlets, and switchplates for, 173
of focal points, 106
general, 162–68, 177
in kitchens, 176
in living rooms, 171–72
options for, 161–62
recessed, 163–64, 177
sconces, 89, 167–68
task, 168–69, 177
torchères, 166–67
track, 162–63, 177
Lightolier PAR-3 lights, 162
Living rooms:
  dining rooms combined with,
  56, 58–61, 115
  lighting in, 171–72
  walk-through, 54–57
Loveseats, 18, 19, 30, 51, 62, 64,
  91, 155
L-shaped configurations, 51
Lucite, 71, 106, 107, 218

M

Marble tables, 40
Men, what to do with, 72–73
Mirrors, 128–29, 145
Miss Rumphius (Cooney), 9
Modular units, 50–53

O

Occupants, number of, 14
Ottomans, 18, 19, 40
Outlets, 173
Owners, 14, 181, 216

P

Paint, 183–86
Pairs, 25, 34–35, 49
  checklist for, 96
  cohesive look and, 88, 89–91
Paper products, 205, 218
Pets, 15
Photographs, 56–57, 83, 107,
  114, 129, 148–50

Pianos, grand, 18, 51, 107
Pillows, 214
  accent, 53
  points-up placement of, 71, 100, 101, 155
  throw, 19, 27, 53, 71, 78, 91, 100, 101, 155
Plants, 153–55
Pottery, Roseville, 140
Presley, Elvis, memorabilia of, 108–11
Priorities, 6
  questionnaire for, 14–15

R

Radiator covers, 198
Reading areas, 65
Recessed lighting, 162–63, 177
Refrigerator magnets, 218
Renters, 13, 14, 181, 216
ReWard, explanation of, 9
Roller coaster effect from differing furniture heights, 6, 37, 43, 66, 79, 80–87, 103
Roosevelt, Theodore, *xiii*
Roseville pottery, 140
Rugs, 188–89, 218
  area, 39, 41, 47
  removal of, 77
  seagrass, 35
  sisal, 51
Runners, 89

S

Sconces, 89, 167–68
"Screaming distance," 16–17, 20–23, 29, 145
Screens, 102–5
Seagrass rugs, 35
Secondary seating areas, 65
Shades and blinds, 189–91

Shell beautification, 181–99
  checklist for, 199
  definition of, 181–82
  floors, rugs, and carpets, 187–89
  paint and wall coverings, 183–87
  top-to-bottom transformation of, 192–97
  window treatments, 189–91
Sisal rugs, 51
Slipcovers, 53, 65
Slipper chairs, 65
Sofa beds, 40, 209
Sofas, 18, 19, 155
  balance and, 64–65, 69
  modular, 50–53, 62
  at 90–degree angles from walls, 56, 62
  placing of, 22, 26, 29, 30, 33, 34, 37, 38, 41, 45, 47, 48, 55, 56, 62, 99, 117
  walking space behind, 45
Storage space, 15, 40, 51, 52, 101
"Stuff." *See* Accessories
Style, comfort and, 66
Switchplates, 173
Symmetry. *See* Pairs

T

Tables. *See also* Coffee tables; End tables
  bedside, 91
  butler's 37–38
  dining, 43, 58–61
  drop-leaf, 56
  kitchen, 43
Task lighting, 168–69, 177
Televisions, 15, 35, 47, 49
Ten most common decorating mistakes, 6

Throw pillows, 19, 27, 71, 78, 91, 100, 101, 155
Tiles, 189
Torchères, 166–67
Towels, 89
Track lighting, 162–63, 177
Traffic flow, 18, 24–27, 43–45, 62
Trees, 30
Trunks, 40

U

Upholstered chairs, 18, 19, 34, 65
Use-What-You-Have Interiors, 3

V

Video equipment, 15
  wall units for, 35, 39, 49

W

Walk-through living rooms, 54–57
"Wallflower" rooms, 42–43, 46–49, 145
Wallpaper, 133, 187, 218
Walls, "isolation" of, 80–81, 84–85, 96
Wall units, 39, 49
  balance and, 67, 79
  as focal points, 18, 35, 97, 100–101, 115
  height of, 86
Ward, Tracy, 9
Window boxes, 155, 218
Windows, 98, 114
Window treatments, 189–91
Wine racks, 158
Wooden chairs, 65
Wood floors, 187–88